The Inscriptions of Calakmul

ROYAL MARRIAGE AT A MAYA CITY IN CAMPECHE, MEXICO

by
Joyce Marcus

Ann Arbor
1987

ISBN 0-915703-15-7

Frontispiece. A strangler fig tightens its grip on a monument at Calakmul.

ACKNOWLEDGMENTS

My thanks go, first of all, to William J. Folan for inviting me to be the epigrapher on his Proyecto Calakmul, and for making my photographic and sketching sessions at the site so productive. In the field, Jacinto May Hau and Patrick Folan helped me rig up the generator and lights to carry out night photography of the Calakmul monuments. Lynda Florey Folan aided me in arranging everything else in Campeche, prior to and after my stay at Calakmul.

Back in the United States, Ian Graham generously supplied me with xerox copies of Eric von Euw's drawings of the Calakmul inscriptions. Von Euw had completed pencil sketches of a number of stelae; these provided an important check against my own sketches of the same inscriptions, my day and night photographs of the monuments, and the drawings and photographs made by Morley and Denison during the 1930s. It is fortunate that the photographs by Morley and Denison were taken when they were, because some of the monuments which today are broken, missing, or deteriorated were in far better condition in Morley's time. In fact, we must return frequently to the work of Morley and Denison to clarify important details in the inscriptions, to work out many of the Initial Series dates, and to ascertain the original location of some monuments. Some of the stelae that were *in situ* in the 1930s are now elsewhere; for example, Stela 51 is in the Museo Nacional de Antropología in Mexico City and Stela 9 is in a Campeche museum. Other monuments apparently have been removed illegally from Mexico -- Stela 53 is in the United States and Stela 89 (minus the hieroglyphic text on the sides which were sawn off by looters) is currently on exhibit in the Rautenstrauch Joest Museum für Völkerkunde in Cologne, West Germany. Still others (such as Stelae 50 and 52) are totally missing.

I thank John Clark for traveling from Michigan to Calakmul for a week of work in December, 1984, in order to rephotograph from different angles some of the same monuments I had previously recorded. Equally importantly, John was able to photograph and sketch many new monuments that had been located by Folan's Proyecto Calakmul mapping crew since my 1983 stay.

Charles Hastings and Kay Clahassey printed all the photographs that are included in this preliminary report. The cover design of a bound captive on a sculptured outcrop at Calakmul was drafted by Kay Clahassey from an Eric von Euw drawing. All other drawings and site plans were redrafted by John Klausmeyer. At every turn Sally Horvath gave me advice on the preparation of this report. Rachael Cohen and Jill Lopick helped me format my manuscript on numerous occasions. All their efforts are greatly appreciated.

TABLE OF CONTENTS

LIST OF FIGURES

LIST OF TABLES

FOREWORD

William J. Folan

Calakmul is a major Maya regional center in southeastern Campeche, Mexico, some 35 kilometers from the border with Guatemala. It has been suggested (Folan 1985, 1987) that Calakmul and nearby El Mirador, Guatemala, may once have been "twin cities" separated by only 37 kilometers. Each of these grand centers may also have played the role of regional capital for an emerging primitive state during the Late Preclassic, thus representing a wellspring for this type of organization in the Maya Lowlands. Structure II of Calakmul and the El Tigre structure of El Mirador represent two very similar public buildings of virtually the same shape and dimensions, suggesting to me not only the shared importance of these cities, but perhaps even their dedication to the same deity or deified royal ancestor. Although it is not necessarily a topic in which Marcus and I are of one mind, I believe in the distinct possibility that the subsequent fall of El Mirador as a major power, as well as the continued rise of Calakmul during the Classic, may have been due in part to differential local climatic and hydraulic conditions experienced by the two centers. The final dedication of Calakmul's Structure I -- with a base even larger than Structure IV of Tikal -- marks the continued development of Calakmul in the Late Classic.

Joyce Marcus has studied state formation since her student days as an anthropologist. Her model of territorial organization in the Maya area and, specifically, in the Calakmul Region (Marcus 1973, 1976; see also Flannery 1972) was one source which helped inspire my research design for the Calakmul Project, formed to provide insights into the hypothetical frontier between the Northern Petén and the Río Bec, Chenes, and Puuc Regions of the Peninsula of Yucatán, while also seeking out additional information on the Maya state. The Calakmul Project has also provided intensive efforts toward a better understanding of Maya urban development through time.

An integral part of this project, independently developed by Marcus, is her attempt to block out the urban development pattern of Calakmul's nucleus by means of its associated hieroglyphic record. This record she divides into a sequence of rulers and of royal marital couples, identifiable through single and multiple stelae which refer to male and female members of the ranking elite and can be associated with specific public architecture. These results reinforce the Calakmul Project's efforts to record and understand the area from the regional level down through the state, urban, civic/ceremonial core, royal family, and royal individual levels. All this is essential if we are going to extend our goals to the very limits of the archaeological information available to us in the field. As an added dimension of this work, it is the intention of the Calakmul Project to investigate the beginnings, limits, and content of the Late Postclassic province of Cehache, and its possible relationship with the northern and southern reaches of the Maya area.

In these days, when scholars like Sabloff (1987) and Sanders (1987) are referring to centers such as Copán, Honduras, as "urban" or "possessing an urban core" -- even when such centers are considerably smaller than the likes of Calakmul and Cobá, Quintana Roo (Folan, Kintz, and Fletcher 1983) -- it seems time to cast aside outdated models for a more realistic look at Maya achievements. In broad terms, we need to reassess state and urban status, as well as the effects that climatic change have made in the development of Maya polities through time (Folan, Gunn, Eaton, and Patch 1983). Not to be overlooked, however, are the finer stratigraphic possibilities offered by strategies such as Marcus' plan for future excavations at Calakmul (this volume), aimed at dividing the 200- to 300-year periods we have been working with down, in some cases, to the life span of a single historic figure.

BIBLIOGRAPHY

Flannery, Kent V.

    1972   The Cultural Evolution of Civilizations. *Annual Review of Ecology and Systematics*, Volume 3, pp. 399-426. Annual Reviews, Inc., Palo Alto, California.

Folan, William J.

    1985   Calakmul, Campeche. Su Centro Urbano, Estado, y Región en Relación al Concepto del Resto de la Gran Mesoamérica. *Información* 9, pp. 161-185. Universidad Autónoma del Sudeste, Campeche, México.

    1987   El Proyecto Calakmul: Su Patrón de Asentamiento y Sus Implicaciones para la Arqueología Maya. *Segundo Coloquio Internacional de Mayistas*, 17 al 22 de agosto, Campeche, Campeche, México.

Folan, William J., Ellen R. Kintz, and Laraine A. Fletcher

    1983   *Coba: A Classic Maya Metropolis*. Academic Press, New York.

Folan, William J., Joel Gunn, Jack D. Eaton, and Robert W. Patch

    1983   Paleoclimatological Patterning in Southern Mesoamerica. *Journal of Field Archaeology*, Volume 10, pp. 453-468.

Marcus, Joyce

    1973   Territorial Organization of the Lowland Classic Maya. *Science*, Volume 180, pp. 911-916.

    1976   *Emblem and State in the Classic Maya Lowlands: An Epigraphic Approach to Territorial Organization*. Dumbarton Oaks, Washington, D.C.

Sabloff, Jeremy A.

    1987   New Perspectives on the History of Ancient Maya Civilization. *Nature*, Volume 326, Number 6110, pp. 242-243.

Sanders, William T.

    1987   Una Reevaluación del Colapso Maya: La Perspectiva desde Copán. *Segundo Coloquio Internacional de Mayistas*, 17 al 22 de agosto, Campeche, Campeche, México.

...don't spend too much time on glyphs --
try to see your problem in broader perspective.

Letter to Marcus from Tatiana Proskouriakoff
(January 10, 1970)

INTRODUCTION

The last 30 years have seen the study of hieroglyphic
texts from a number of Classic Maya centers such as Piedras Negras,
Yaxchilán, Tikal, Copán, Quiriguá, and Palenque. Many of these
studies follow in the footsteps of Tatiana Proskouriakoff (1960, 1961a,
1961b, 1963, 1964, 1973) and Heinrich Berlin (1955, 1958, 1959,
1960a, 1960b, 1963, 1965, 1968a, 1968b, 1973, 1977, 1982), the first
two epigraphers to open the "door to Maya history". Scholars since
Berlin and Proskouriakoff have succeeded in identifying rulers' names,
the dates of their birth, their accession to the throne, their marriages,
and their deaths. Epigraphers also have established dynastic
sequences and identified site or place names. Most hieroglyphic studies

that were carried out in the 1960s and early 1970s aimed at reconstructing the chronology of events and the sequence of rulers at individual sites. This "site-specific" focus is still with us, and continues to be an important component in our understanding of the history and development of individual Maya sites.

In the 1970s a second focus, that of establishing regional site hierarchies and documenting site interactions, was just beginning (e.g. Marcus 1973, 1974a, 1976b; Adams 1977; Adams and Jones 1981). In this second approach, hieroglyphic inscriptions were employed not so much to reconstruct the events in the life of a particular ruler at one site, as to link individual sites to others with which they interacted. One of the specific goals of such analyses was to understand the nature of Maya territorial organization. During this same period, questions regarding the political evolution of the Maya state were addressed using hieroglyphic texts as a source of primary data. Site interactions in the form of marriage and military alliances, raiding or conquests, elite gift-giving, boat trips by rulers, and attendance at funerals of royalty were documented in the inscriptions. So were changes in regional hierarchies, such as lower-order sites which eventually moved up in the regional hierarchy, and sites that seem to have gained their independence from a center that formerly subjugated them. Such interaction among sites now constitutes an important focus of hieroglyphic studies, and of Maya archaeology in general.

Nearly all the Late Classic Maya centers that have been singled out for long-term excavation have been sites with a large number of hieroglyphic monuments. Ironically, however, the Maya site which may have the single greatest number of stone monuments -- Calakmul -- had not been subjected to nearly as much study until the recent work of William J. Folan and other members of his project (Folan and May Hau 1984; Fletcher, May Hau, Folan, and Folan 1987). Much more extensive work had been carried out at other primary centers, such as Tikal (Shook 1960; Shook, W. R. Coe, Broman, and Satterthwaite 1958; Carr and Hazard 1961; W. R. Coe 1962, 1965a, 1965b, and 1967; Haviland 1967, 1970, 1977, and 1981; Puleston 1974; Puleston and Callender 1967; Fry and Cox 1974); Palenque (Ruz Lhuillier 1952a, 1952b, 1954, 1955, 1958a, 1958b, 1958c, 1958d, 1962, and 1977; Rands and Rands 1959; Acosta 1977); and Copán (Gordon 1896; Longyear 1952; Willey and Leventhal 1979; Leventhal 1979; Willey, Leventhal, and Fash 1978; Baudez 1978a, 1978b, 1979a, and 1979b).

Notwithstanding the fact that no long-term excavation or mapping had been undertaken at Calakmul, it is still surprising that its numerous stone monuments were not the object of more extensive study. There appear to be at least two reasons for this. One is that many of the stelae are in very poor condition, discouraging epigraphers from trying to tease out data from the weathered hieroglyphic texts. The damage from rainwater, lichens, moss, vines, and roots has been such that only Morley, in his zeal to record all Maya dates, was not discouraged. The effects of the natural elements are even more noteworthy at Calakmul than most places because (as Morley and Denison noted) the stelae are made from a rather poor quality, porous limestone which characterizes some of Calakmul's dependencies as well. A second reason sometimes given for the lack of study of the Calakmul inscriptions is the relative inaccessibility of the site. However, it seems likely this inaccessibility would not have discouraged epigraphers were the monuments in better condition.

Even though Calakmul's monuments have suffered considerable weathering during their 1100 - 1500 years, there is still a great deal that can be learned from them, especially if we employ a *contextual* approach. Such an approach is particularly appropriate at Calakmul because there are such clear patterns in the way the Maya placed the monuments. Such patterning in placement, context, and associations was preserved for Lundell, Morley, Bolles, and Denison to recover in the early 1930s.

Like the elite at many other Maya centers, the rulers of Calakmul maintained their dynastic and genealogical records on stelae that were displayed in particular locations: in the case of Calakmul, these dynastic records were placed in association with individual temples in particular plaza groups. The association of a particular ruler's monuments with particular temples is an important element in the *contextual* approach. Clear patterning is revealed in these associations. Lines of dated monuments were set up in front of different temples in plaza groups. Each ruler's dated stelae recorded his personal history and the events that occurred during his reign. The dedication of each ruler's dated monuments also appears to date the dedication, enlargement, or renovation of at least one structure during his reign. Thus, it appears that nearly every Calakmul ruler is associated not only with a set of stelae, but also with at least one temple completed during his reign. The results of our *contextual* analysis will be discussed at length below.

The most significant circumstance that allows us to document the associations between lines of dated monuments and particular structures is the fact that there was very little prehispanic relocation of stelae. Unlike the Maya at other sites (such as Tikal), those at Calakmul rarely reset, damaged, or buried the monuments of earlier rulers. Attempting to explain such differences between sites -- continued public display of earlier rulers' monuments *versus* intentional destruction, burying, or resetting -- could prove to be a fruitful line of investigation. As we will see, this preservation of associations and contexts at Calakmul aids us immeasurably in the kinds of analyses we will do later on.

Finally, we are still able to document this patterning because Calakmul's relative inaccessibility had kept many looters (as well as tourists) from visiting the site. This means that most of the stelae remain in the same places they occupied when Lundell, Morley, Bolles, and Denison first recorded their locations in the 1930s, although there are a few recent exceptions such as those indicated above.

EARLY RESEARCH IN CAMPECHE AND AT THE SITE OF CALAKMUL

On December 29, 1931 Cyrus Lundell, while working for a chicle company in southern Campeche, Mexico, discovered a site which he named *ca* (two), *lak* (adjacent), *mul* (artificial mound), or "Place of Two Adjacent Mounds" (Lundell 1933:152). Lundell drafted a map showing the locations of structures and stelae in their plaza groups, and took a set of photographs; he passed these along to James C. Brydon, who worked for the same company. Shortly thereafter, Brydon showed the material to Dr. John C. Merriam, President of the Carnegie Institution of Washington, while both of them were aboard a boat bound for New Orleans.

In March of 1932, Lundell traveled to Chichén Itzá where Sylvanus Morley was working. Lundell informed him of a newly-discovered, very impressive site that included large numbers of carved stelae with legible dates.   Morley, always excited about recording calendric information from newly-discovered stelae, was eager to visit Lundell's site; he therefore requested permission of the Departamento de Monumentos Prehispánicos, which was granted by Ignacio Marquina.   Thus in April, 1932 the first expedition to Calakmul set out. It was led by Morley, accompanied by Karl Ruppert (archaeologist), John S. Bolles (architect and surveyor), Gustav Strömsvik (engineer), and Mrs. Morley (in charge of the camp "commissary").

Morley describes the first afternoon at the site (April 9, 1932) as one devoted to setting up camp. Then he states:

> the following day was one of the most remarkable in the writer's twenty-five years of tropical exploration. With the Lundell sketch map as a guide, the institution party set out to explore the area covered by the map. Lundell had enumerated 64 stelae, or sculptured hieroglyphic monuments, of which the expedition was able to find all but two. One of the missing two was the unsculptured rectangular altar on the summit of the substructure supporting the middle building of Structure D [designated Structure IVb on Bolles' map; see Figure 3 in this report], which Lundell had mistaken for a sculptured stela; the other was not found in the position indicated on his sketch map and it appears probable that he must have confused it with some other stela already accounted for elsewhere. This reduced the total of stelae found by Lundell to 62.

> The Carnegie Institution's Calakmul expedition, during the 15 days it was at the site, discovered 41 additional stelae, bringing the total of known stelae at this site to 103, the largest number by 27 per cent, yet reported from any city of the Maya civilization (Morley 1933:195).

Between 1932 and 1938, the Division of Historical Research of the Carnegie Institution of Washington sent out four expeditions to Calakmul, including the one described above by Morley. On the first expedition, Morley had been the project epigrapher; however, on the second, third, and fourth expeditions John H. Denison, Jr. served in that capacity, with Morley generously supplying Denison with a copy of all his notes on the Calakmul inscriptions.

Both Morley and Denison carried out exceptional work on the stelae of Calakmul under very difficult circumstances. During the first expedition Morley devoted himself to recording all the dates and calendric information on the monuments; most of those dates have been confirmed by more recent work (Marcus 1970, 1974a, 1983b). It is unfortunate that Morley was less interested in recording the non-calendric portions of the texts, since the damage and deterioration of the last 50 years have made many of these data unrecoverable. This loss is particularly felt nowadays, when we are able to extract so much more dynastic and genealogical information from the inscriptions than was possible in Morley's day.

In addition to work at Calakmul proper, the staff of the four Carnegie Institution expeditions studied many other sites in the vicinity. In particular, J. P. O'Neill (in 1933) and F. P. Parris (in 1934) mapped several sites that were evidently part of Calakmul's realm. Many of these were secondary centers, and all apparently functioned as lower-order dependencies.

In addition to an important Calakmul site map prepared by Bolles (and redrawn here as Figure 3), the four Campeche expeditions drafted maps for many of the other ruins in southern Campeche. For example, O'Neill mapped the ruins of La Muñeca, Nochebuena, Río Bec (Group I), Hormiguero, Alta Mira, and Naachtún; Parris prepared maps for Oxpemul, Uaacbal, Becán, Channá, Río Bec (Group II - V), Balakbal, Pared de los Reyes, and Uxul. In 1938, Shepherd added maps of Okolhuitz, Xpuhil, Culucbalom, Pechal, and Peor es Nada.

It would be difficult to overestimate the Carnegie Institution of Washington's work in southern Campeche and throughout the Maya area. In many regions their work, in both quantity and quality, may never be surpassed.

CALAKMUL: THE SITE AND ITS SETTING

Calakmul is a huge Maya center located in the southeastern part of the modern Mexican state of Campeche -- specifically, in the southwestern part of the Yucatán Peninsula at 18° 05' North and 89° 49' West (see Figure 1). Aerial photographs reveal that the central part of Calakmul is encircled by an interconnected set of canals, *bajos*, and *acalches*; the area thus enclosed is approximately 20 square kilometers. In a map published by Morley (1937, Volume V, Part 2: Plate 179) a huge depression labeled "Bajo de Calakmul" is shown immediately to the west of the site, trending from northwest to southeast and occupying an area perhaps 35 x 20 kilometers (see Figure 2).

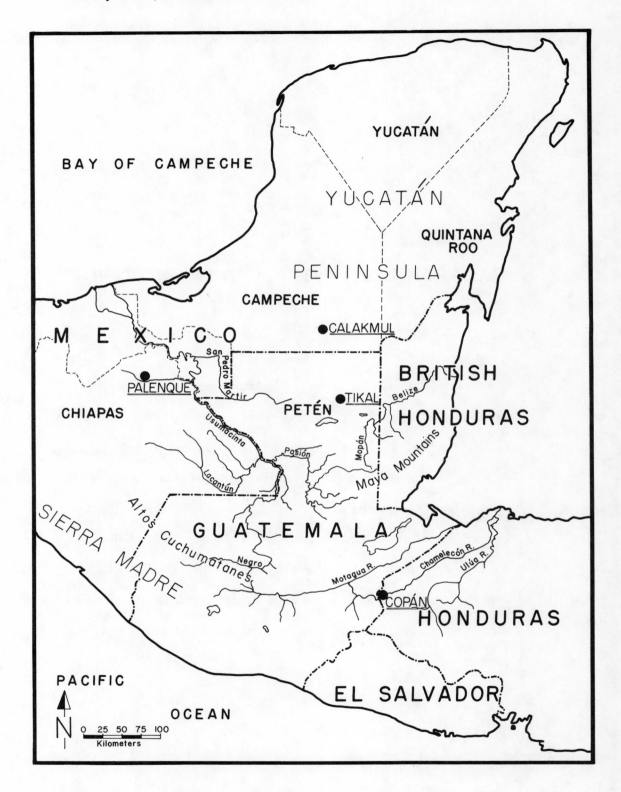

1. Map of the Maya region, showing Calakmul in southern Campeche, Mexico.

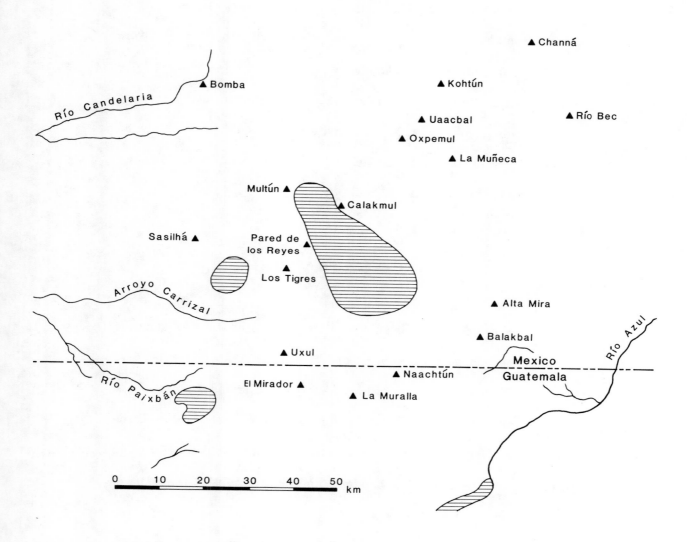

2. Immediately to the west of Calakmul is a huge depression called the "Bajo de Calakmul", here shown shaded with horizontal lines. Other *bajos* are designated in the same manner.

As is characteristic of many other Maya cities, the monumental public buildings (temples, palaces, and platforms) occupy the "downtown" or central sector of Calakmul; this sector covers approximately 1.75 square kilometers. Nearly all the stelae are to be found within this downtown area, although important new stone monuments (some carved in the round on small boulders and a few on extremely large ones) have been found further out from the site's center by Folan's project.

MAPPING STRATEGIES

Not surprisingly, the map prepared by Bolles in the 1930s and published by Ruppert and Denison in 1943 (Plate 61) does not extend beyond the downtown sector which includes most of the stelae and public buildings (see Figure 3 of this report). During the 1930s, all Carnegie Institution projects concentrated their efforts on mapping the zone of public buildings and plaza groups at the heart of Maya centers. However, while Lundell and Bolles sought to map the downtown area, Folan's Proyecto Calakmul has additional goals: (1) discovering the limits of Calakmul itself, (2) mapping the area between Calakmul and its satellites or dependent communities, and (3) locating the limits of the Calakmul "realm" or polity. With those goals in mind, since 1982 Folan's project has been mapping an area that now encompasses over 30 square kilometers (Fletcher, May Hau, Folan, and Folan 1987; Folan, personal communication 1986). In this larger area, some 6250 structures have been located so far. The population estimate for the entire city of Calakmul is 50,000 people (Fletcher, May Hau, Folan, and Folan 1987).

The principal natural feature affecting the location and distribution of structures at the site (and presumably a factor in its having been selected for settlement in the first place) is the huge *bajo* immediately to the west of the site center. There is reason to believe that the earliest structures may be concentrated on the land nearest the bajo (Figure 2). This huge depression was first described by Lundell (1933:153) and later included on a map published by Morley (1937, Volume V, Part 2: Plate 179). It is significant that hydraulic features, including canals, also appear to have surrounded the downtown area.

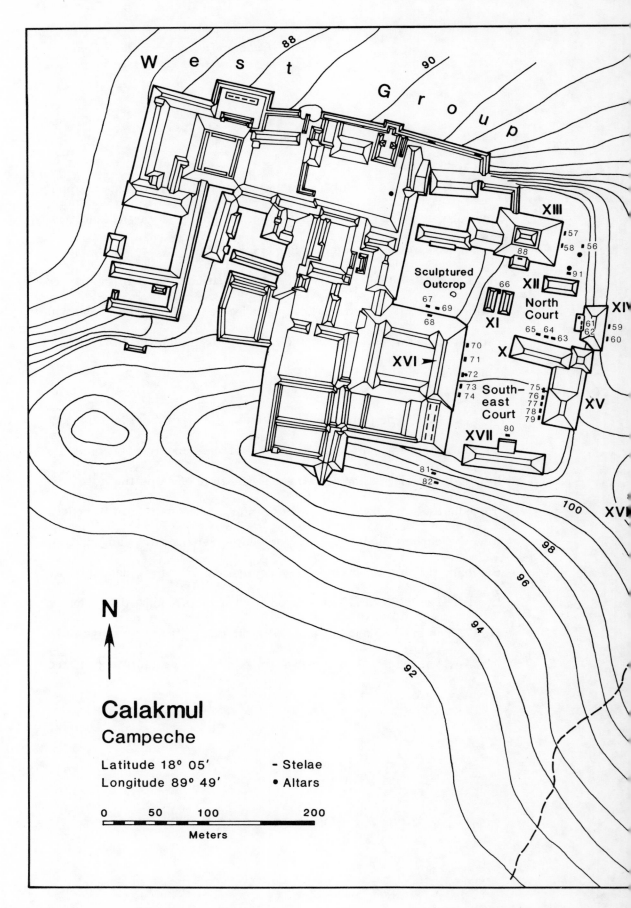

3. Map of "downtown" Calakmul, drafted by J. S. Bolles in the 1930s, showing numbered stelae

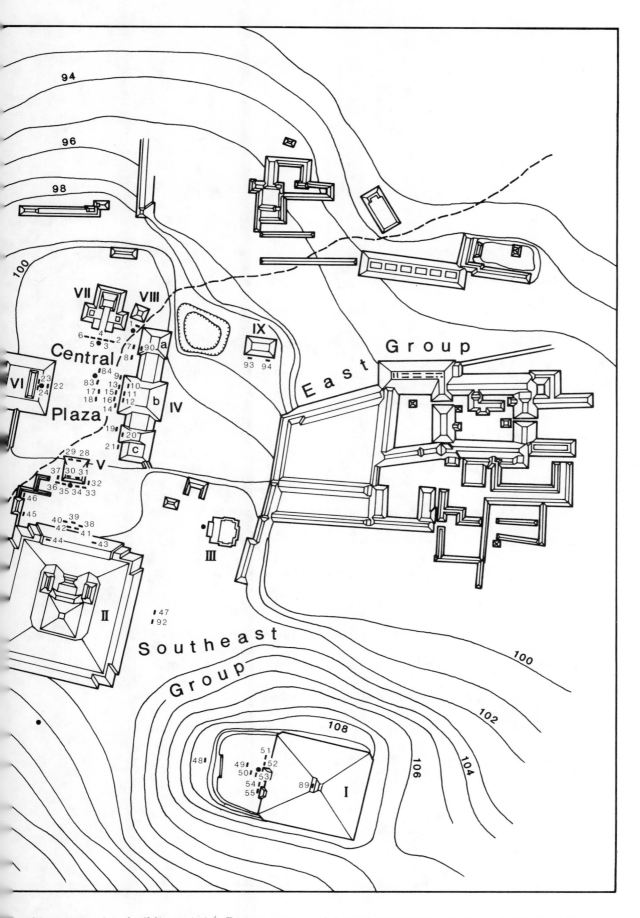

Arabic numerals), buildings (with Roman numerals), and unnumbered altars (redrafted from
rt and Denison 1943: Plate 61).

This central area (Figure 3) is on well-drained higher ground (34 meters higher than the surrounding *bajo*, according to Folan's recent topographic work); however, it is still within close proximity to the *bajos*, *aguadas*, and hydraulic features. Many other Maya sites -- including Tikal, Naachtún, Uaxactún, El Mirador, Xultún, Naranjo, Nakum, Kinal, Kohunlich, and Tzibanche -- are located near to or at the edge of large *bajos* (see Harrison 1977:491; Adams, Brown, and Culbert 1981:1462). Many of these sites can be seen in Figure 4.

Downtown Calakmul includes nearly 1000 buildings and features of the type we have come to expect at Classic Maya sites, particularly those that served as regional capitals or primary centers for their districts: huge plazas, temples, stelae, ballcourts, palaces, pyramids, and platforms. The map drafted by Bolles (Ruppert and Denison 1943: Plate 61) was used by Ruppert to divide this downtown sector into four complexes of structures (called "groups") that surround the Central Plaza; these were designated the Southeast Group, the West Group, the East Group, and the Northeast Group. Let us now look at these divisions in more detail.

4. Maya sites in the Department of Petén, Guatemala; Belize; and Campeche, Mexico.

THE CENTRAL PLAZA

Moving clockwise from the north, the Central Plaza is delimited by Structures VII, VIII, IV, V, and VI (see Figure 3). We begin in the north with Structure VII, noting the arrangement of five stelae in front of the structure in an orderly line (Stelae 6, 5, 4, 3, and 2); in the center of that line is a circular altar, placed in front of Stela 4. All the monuments appear to be plain. A small temple (*circa* 8.8 x 4.8 meters) was built atop Structure VII, a 24-meter high substructure.

At the northeast corner of the plaza lies Structure VIII, approximately six meters high and associated with only one stela (Stela 1) and altar.

Moving to the east side of the plaza, we find Structure IV. Atop its long platform are three separate structures labeled *a*, *b*, and *c*; each appears to have a stairway on its west side. Associated with the northernmost structure (*a*) were Stelae 7 and 8 (set up to the southwest) and Stela 90 (on the slope south of the stairway). The southernmost structure (*c*) was associated with Stelae 19, 20, and 21. The central structure (*b*) is the most impressive of the three in both size and in the number of associated stelae (which are arranged in three rows). In the back row are three apparently plain stelae -- Stelae 10, 11, and 12; in the middle row are Stelae 9, 13, 15, 16, and 14; and in the front row are Stelae 17 and 18. Still further out in the plaza to the northwest are Stelae 83 and 84, with a circular altar set near the latter.

The central structure just described (Structure IVb) is apparently a two-room temple (see Figure 5) and is clearly associated with the largest number of stelae of any of the three structures on the platform. When mapped by Ruppert and Bolles in the 1930s, the inner and outer room of this temple were filled with 1 - 2 meters of debris, mostly roof and upper wall fall.

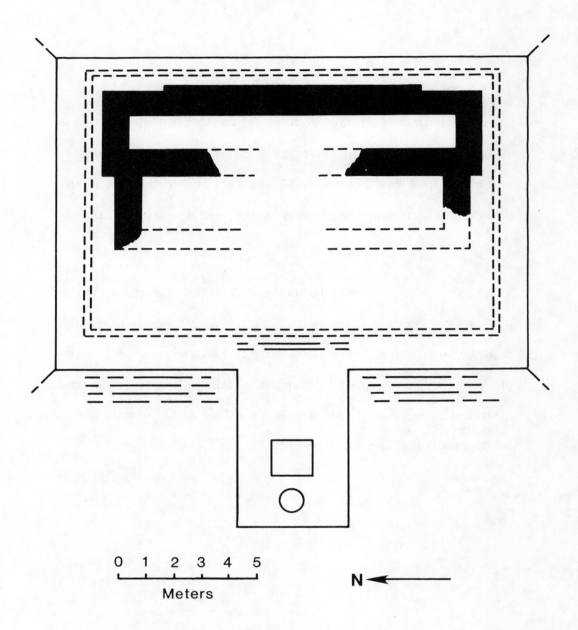

5. A two-room temple (Structure IVb) sits atop a centrally-located platform delimiting the east side of the Central Plaza at Calakmul (redrafted from Ruppert and Denison 1943: Figure 15).

At the south end of the Central Plaza lies Structure V. On the south side of the structure at the base of an apparent stairway is a round altar; to the east are Stelae 34, 33, and around the southeast corner (to the north) is Stela 32. To the west of the centrally-located altar are Stelae 35 and 36, and around the southwest corner (to the north) is Stela 37. Atop the southern part of Structure V itself are two apparently plain stelae (Nos. 30 and 31). To the north of the structure are two paired stelae (Stelae 28 and 29).

Northwest of Structure V lies Structure VI, which Ruppert (1943:20) compared to Structure VII in Group E at Uaxactún. Associated with the east side of Structure VI are three stelae and an altar. Stela 22 stands by itself near the base of the structure; near the top of the building stand Stelae 23 and 24; and between the latter two stelae is a small, circular plain altar. On the west side of Structure VI are three more stelae (Stelae 25, 26, and 27), with a centrally-placed plain, round altar set in front of Stela 26.

THE SOUTHEAST GROUP

The Southeast Group includes Structures I, II, and III. Structure I faces to the west (toward the southeast corner of Structure II). On top of Structure I's pyramidal base is a flat area measuring approximately 12 x 14 meters which supports a four-meter-high mound; Stela 89 was set up on the west side of this mound. When I photographed this stela in 1983, it had been cut into several fragments by looters, and I was able to locate only a few sections of the text that once comprised the sides of the monument. Fortunately, the intact text had been photographed first by Morley (1933:201) and later by Ruppert and Denison (1943: Plate 53c).

On a terrace to the west side of Structure I were Stelae 51, 52, 53, 54, 55 (from north to south in the back row). In front of Stela 53 appeared Stela 50, and to the northwest was a plain stela (Stela 49). Still further to the west, but below the terrace, was Stela 48. The figure depicted on Stela 89 faced north, as did the figures on Stelae 51, 53, 54, and 48. In contrast, the male figure on Stela 52 faced south in order to gaze at the individual depicted on Stela 54, who was apparently his wife. The carving on Stela 55 is too weathered to reveal what direction the figure faced. (See Figure 3 for the locations of all Structure I stelae).

Structure II is the largest and tallest at Calakmul, with an approximate height of 50 meters (see Figure 6). [Structure I is the second largest and tallest, also roughly 50 meters in height, but appears somewhat taller since it is built on a higher promontory than Structure II.] The Structure II pyramid faces north, with seven stelae set up on this north face. Five stelae were set up at the base of the pyramid (38, 39, and 40 in the front row, and 41 and 42 in the back row). On two different terraces (or steps of a broad stairway?) are Stela 43 (on a lower terrace, east end) and Stela 44 (on a higher terrace, west end). This broad basal stairway (perhaps nearly seventy meters in width) does not appear to have continued to the top of the pyramid; rather, it seems to have narrowed into a stairway of less than ten meters in width. This narrower stairway led to the top of the pyramid, which measures approximately 60 x 70 meters and features four structures. Three of the structures are lined up in the northern portion, while a large pyramid rises behind them in the southern portion. Two plain stelae (Stelae 47 and 92) were set up on the east side of Structure II.

6. View of Structure II, Calakmul (taken from the top of Structure I).

To the northwest of Structure II stood Stela 45, which was set up to the east of a small mound. Just to the north of this small mound, Stela 46 was erected.

To the northeast of Structure II lies Structure III (Morley 1933:202-203). This well-preserved structure, set atop a five-meter-high platform, is small when compared to the massive volume of the pyramidal substructures of Structures I and II. However, because of its exceptional preservation, Structure III provides us with one of our few Calakmul floor plans (see Figure 7).

Structure III is now a twelve-room building with much of its upper structure present. One can see vaulted rooms, capstones, roof beams, and the kinds of architectural detail most often fallen and destroyed. Its layout reveals a nearly bilaterally symmetrical plan which is similar to "small elite palaces" at other Maya centers. Structure III's only stairway is on the west side; the location of the twelve rooms and stairway are given in Figure 7.

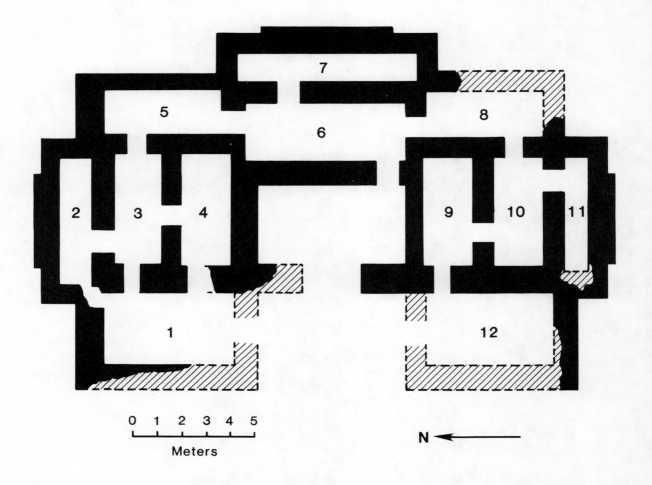

7. Structure III, a twelve-room palace at Calakmul (redrafted from Ruppert and Denison 1943: Figure 2).

Room 1 (3.05 x 5.25 meters) has two walls still standing on its north and east sides. There are four doorways allowing entry into and exit from Room 1, making it one of the most accessible rooms in the building.

Room 2 is long and narrow (approximately 1.30 x 5.30 meters). Its north wall exhibits nine "ventilators" or small window-like openings; four are at floor level (Ventilators 1-4), one is near the center of the wall (Ventilator 5), and four are near the top of the wall (Ventilators 6-9) [see Ruppert and Denison 1943: Figure 6b]. Ventilator 5 (32 x 30 centimeters in size) is located 70 centimeters above the floor. (To the west of this ventilator, Lundell scratched his name into the plaster wall with the date 12-29-31, the day he discovered Calakmul.) The east wall has two more ventilators, one at floor level and the other two meters above the floor.

The doorway leading from Room 2 to Room 3 still had most of its lintel intact when Lundell, Ruppert, and Denison visited the site. However, even then one of its four wooden sections was missing. Two cordholders (which probably allowed a door, such as a drapery made of perishable materials, to be held in place or drawn aside) were present on either side of the doorway in the south wall of Room 2

(*Ibid*.: Figure 7). Room 3 communicates with Rooms 1, 2, and 4; the capstone and vault are largely intact.

The north, west, and south walls of Room 4 have partially collapsed. Room 4 has two doorways, one with access to Room 1, and the other to Room 3. Room 5 also has two doorways, thereby communicating with Rooms 3 and 6. Room 6, in turn, has four doorways, giving access to Rooms 5, 7, 8, and the central patio to the west. The doorway leading into the patio could be sealed off by some drapery of perishable material hung and held in place by cords attached to either side.

Room 7 is one of the most inaccessible in the palace; the only entrance into the room is through Room 6. As for Room 8, its walls have nearly collapsed. In contrast, Room 9 is still in good condition. The stone vault of the room rises over two meters, and the capstones have a span of 27 centimeters and are on the same level as those in Room 10 (*Ibid*.: Figure 11). Room 9 has two doorways, communicating with Rooms 10 and 12.

Room 10 has three doorways, communicating with Rooms 8, 9, and 11. Three of the four wooden beams that form the lintel still remain in the doorway leading to Room 11 (*Ibid*.: Figure 13).

Sockets that were made in the jambs to either side of the doorway suggest that a pole may have been inserted there for the purpose of holding a curtain to create privacy for the occupants of the room.

Room 11 has only one doorway, giving access to Room 10 (*Ibid.*: Figure 14); Room 12 is in poor condition, but appears to have had dimensions similar to those of Room 1. What became the central patio was originally a room whose vaulted ceiling had collapsed, evidently sometime during the use of the structure; apparently the walls were then leveled off to create a raised central patio.

THE WEST GROUP

The West Group is divided into a number of courts and patios. In the eastern sector of the West Group are two large courts, designated North Court and Southeast Court; separating these two courts is Structure X (see Figure 3). On the north side of Structure X are three stelae (Nos. 63, 64, and 65).

Structure XI is a ballcourt within the North Court. At the north end of the ballcourt is a stela fragment (Stela 66) that was re-used in the facing of the west bench (see Figure 8).

Structure XII is in the northeastern part of the North Court. To the north of this structure is Stela 91, associated with a small round altar. Structure XIII constitutes the northern limit of the North Court. On a terrace on the south face of Structure XIII a stela nearly 4.5 meters tall was erected (Stela 88). East of Structure XIII three stelae (Nos. 57, 58, and 56) and one altar were placed.

8. Stela 66, found in the west bench of the ball court (Structure XI), is the lower portion of a monument that includes only the legs of a figure.

Structure XIV defines the east side of the North Court, while Structure XV (southeast of Structure X) defines the east side of the Southeast Court. On the west side of Structure XIV three stone monuments were set up: a plain round altar, Stela 61, and Stela 62. On the east side of Structure XIV, Stelae 59 and 60 were erected. To the west of Structure XV five stelae were erected: Stelae 75, 76, 77, 78, and 79.

Structure XVI lies on the west side of the Southeast Court. Set up in front of Structure XVI were Stelae 74, 73, 72 (with an associated round altar), 71, and 70. Structure XVII is located on the south side of the Southeast Court. Only one stela (Stela 80) was set up in front of its stairway (on the north side of the structure). In addition, two plain stelae (Nos. 81 and 82) were set up to the southwest of Structure XVII.

Lying to the southeast of Structure XVII is Structure XVIII; on its north side are Stelae 85, 86, and 87.

SCULPTURED OUTCROP

West of the ballcourt (Structure XI) and north of Structure XVI (and Stelae 67, 68, and 69), one of Bolles' workmen found a bedrock sculpture of seven captives with their arms bound behind their back. Shown on the cover of this report is one of these nude figures with his arms tied back with rope (redrawn from Eric von Euw's original sketch). Associated with one of the other nude captives is a short text of three eroded hieroglyphs that may give the name of the captive. Today the exposed area of carved bedrock measures approximately 5 by 5.5 meters. Morley (1933:204) gave the dimensions as "17 feet by 21 feet" and Denison (1943:122) gave them as 5.18 by 6.39 meters. A similar sculpture which includes two life-size bound captives was found on a rectangular outcrop of limestone along the course of the Maler causeway at Tikal (W. R. Coe 1967:84). No doubt many other bedrock sculptures remain to be uncovered at other primary centers.

THE EAST GROUP

The East Group lies directly east of the Central Plaza and appears to include no stelae. This area seems to have been a complex of palaces and other elite residences that delimit interior patios and courts. Future excavations in this area could provide us with important data on elite residences, thereby allowing us to compare Calakmul elite to those living at Tikal and other centers.

THE NORTHEAST GROUP

The Northeast Group is located approximately 900 meters to the northeast of Structure II (see Figure 9). Nine stelae and a plain altar were located here. On the east side of the plaza is a large pyramidal structure; set up in front of it are Stelae 99, 98, 97, 96, a plain altar, and Stela 95. On the north side of the same plaza is another line of stelae (Nos. 103, 102, 101, and 100).

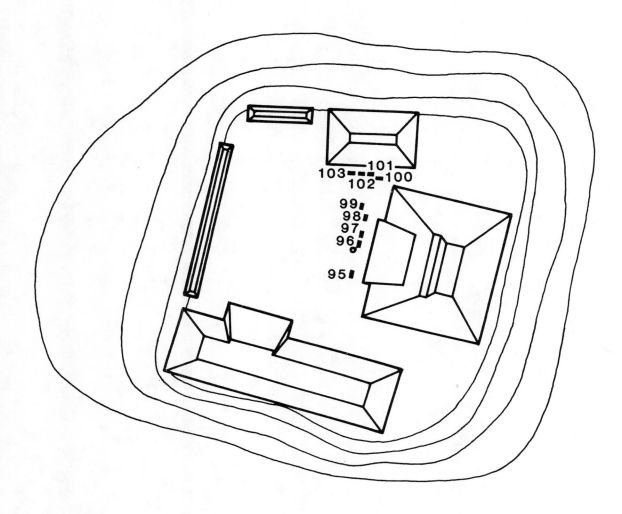

9. The Northeast Group, set atop a promontory approximately 900 meters north of Structure II. This group includes five buildings, two of which are associated with rows of stelae. Associated with the eastern building are Stelae 95-99; associated with the northeast building are Stelae 100-103 (redrafted from Ruppert and Denison 1943: Plate 61).

OTHER GROUPS

Monuments 104, 105, 106, and 107 were found in a plaza group 130 meters west of the Northeast Group (see Figures 10 and 11). Centrally placed atop this plaza group's northernmost structure was Monument 104; set up in front of the same structure were Monuments 106 and 105 (for the latter, see Figures 12 and 13). Further to the south was Monument 107, with an associated altar (see Figure 11).

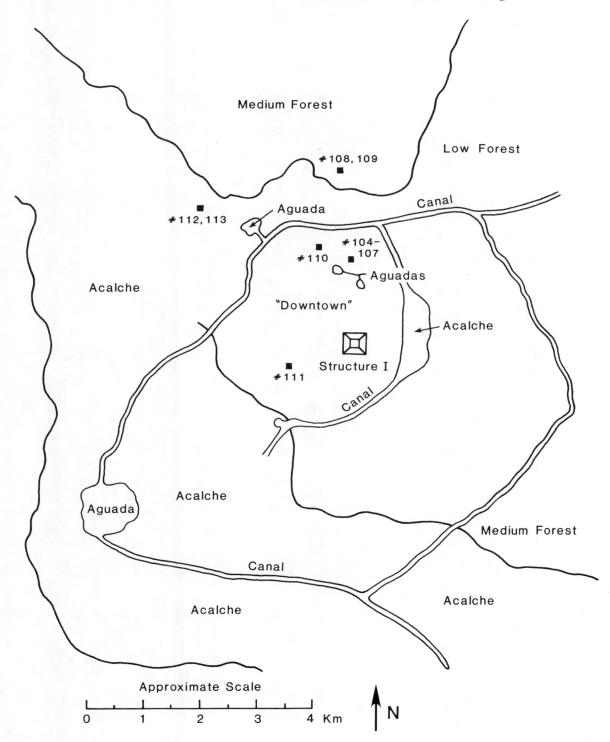

10. While most of the Calakmul stelae were found in the "downtown" sector of the site, other stone monuments were discovered outside that area. Note that the downtown area is encircled by concentric rings of canals and associated hydraulic works (redrafted from a 1984 sketch map prepared by Jacinto May Hau and William J. Folan).

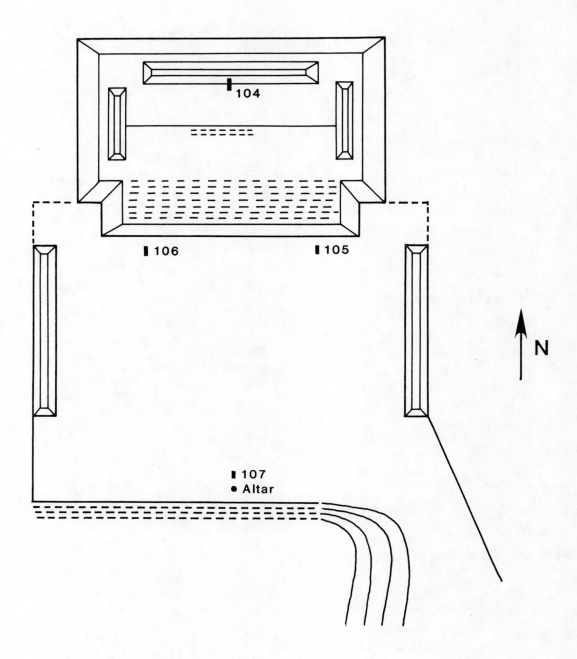

11. Sketch map of a plaza group approximately 130 meters west of the Northeast Group, showing locations of Stelae 104; 105; 106; and 107, with its associated altar (redrafted from map prepared by John Clark).

12. Monument 105, located in a plaza group approximately 130 meters west of the Northeast Group.

13. Closeup of text on Monument 105.

Monuments 108 and 109 (Figures 14 and 15) were found on a small rectangular structure located approximately three kilometers to the north of the center of the site. Monument 108 (Figure 14) was associated with a small, round stone altar. Other plain stelae were located in mound groups near Monuments 108 and 109, but were not assigned numbers. Had all plain stelae and any plain altars been numbered, we would conservatively be able to assign 140 numbers to stone monuments at Calakmul.

Monuments 110 and 111 (Figures 16 and 17) were originally called "monos" by the Calakmul workmen; unlike stelae, they are boulder sculptures carved in the round. Both monuments are located on mounds, and resemble crude boulder sculptures known from other Maya sites (e.g. Copán, see Gordon 1896; Tikal, see Miscellaneous Sculpture 82). Monument 110 is located to the north of the Central Plaza, while Monument 111 is located to the south (see Figure 10).

14.   Monument 108 and its associated altar were found on a small mound approximately three kilometers north of "downtown" Calakmul (see Figure 10).

15. Monument 109, Calakmul.

16. Monument 110, Calakmul.

17. Monument 111, Calakmul.

18. Monument 112, Calakmul.

19. Monument 113, Calakmul.

Approximately three kilometers northwest of the site center Monuments 112 and 113 were discovered (Figure 10). Both were located within the same plaza in a mound group. Like Monuments 110 and 111, Monument 112 is a rather crude carving (Figure 18).

Monument 113 is a small sculpture (approximately one meter in maximum dimension) featuring a deep U-shaped groove with a shallower groove pecked into it (see Figure 19). Below these grooves are four small, shallow, circular depressions. The monument was found in association with a well-worn basin metate.

CALAKMUL MONUMENTS: EPIGRAPHY AND ICONOGRAPHY

Calakmul, as we mentioned above, can lay claim to the largest corpus of stelae of any Classic Maya site. In 1931 Lundell located 62 stelae; in 1932 Morley increased this number to 103; and Folan's project during 1982-1986 increased this total to at least 113. If we also include the miscellaneous plain stelae and altars that have been found since Morley's and Denison's investigations, the number exceeds 140.

Of the 103 stelae recorded originally by Morley, at least 79 had been carved, and many of these on three or four sides. Morley was successful in working out fifty-one Initial Series dates at Calakmul. Some of the more eroded stelae showed little more than Initial Series dates that began lengthy, but largely illegible hieroglyphic inscriptions; others in better condition revealed royal figures on the front face and less-weathered hieroglyphic texts on the sides. For some of the weathered inscriptions, night photography often revealed details that can not be seen in photographs taken in daylight (see Figure 20).

Calakmul stelae span the years A.D. 514 to 830, but unfortunately the 316-year record is not an uninterrupted one. The longest gap is early in the sequence: following the carving of a ruler and hieroglyphic text on Stela 43 in A.D. 514, there was a 109-year gap until the next monument was carved. There are at least two possible explanations for this gap: either no monuments were carved during this period, or else we are missing the intervening monuments because they were destroyed or removed from view by later rulers. This gap or hiatus is part of a widespread Petén phenomenon in which there is not only a marked decrease in the number of stelae carved, but also a noticeable drop in the number of public buildings constructed (Willey 1974 and 1977).

20. Comparison of daylight (L.) and night (R.) photography of the same Calakmul monument, Stela 29. Each photo reveals different details.

The 316-year span of Calakmul's stelae may eventually be lengthened at both its early and late ends. It would not be surprising if future work uncovers monuments predating the A.D. 514 stela; and at the late end, we already have a few candidates for stelae that, on iconographic and stylistic grounds, may have been carved after A.D. 830. A preliminary study of the iconography on some stelae that have poorly preserved Initial Series dates (Marcus 1970, 1983b) suggests that these monuments belong stylistically to early Cycle 10 (A.D. 830-850?).

By excerpting from Morley's (1933) and Denison's (1943) published work, we are able to present the following table of dates from Calakmul.

Table 1. Long Count Dates Reported from Calakmul

Monument	Long Count Date	Kind of Date
St. 43	9. 4. 0. 0 .0	Initial Series
St. 28	9. 9.10. 0. 0	Initial Series
St. 29	9. 9.10. 0. 0	Initial Series
St. 1	9.10. 0. ?. 5	Initial Series
St. 9	9.10.16.16.19	Initial Series
St. 32	9.11. 5. 0. 0	Initial Series
St. 33	9.11. 5. 0. 0	Initial Series
St. 35	9.11. 8.10. 0	Initial Series
(St. 35)	9.11.10. 0. 0	Initial Series
St. 36	9.11.10. 0. 0	Initial Series
St. 88	9.11. ?. ?. ?	Style Dating
(St. 9)	9.11.10. 0. 0	Initial Series
(St. 9)	9.12. 0. 0. 0	Period-Ending
St. 13	9.12. 0. 0. 0	Initial Series
St. 74	9.12. 0. 0.0?	Initial Series
St. 75	9.12. 0. 0. 0	Initial Series
St. 86	9.12. 0. 0. 0	Initial Series
St. 76	9.12. 5. 0. 0	Initial Series
St. 70	9.12. 8. 9. 9	Initial Series
St. 77	9.12.10. 0. 0	Initial Series
St. 93	9.12.10. 0. 0	Initial Series
St. 94	9.12.10. 0. 0	Initial Series
St. 79	9.13. 0. 0.0?	Initial Series
St. 23	9.13.10. 0. 0	Initial Series
St. 24	9.13.10. 0. 0	Initial Series
St. 38	9.13.10. 0.0?	Initial Series
St. 40	9.13.10. 0. 0	Initial Series
St. 41	9.13.10. 0. 0	Initial Series
St. 71	9.14. 0. 0. 0	Initial Series
St. 72	9.14. 0. 0. 0	Initial Series
St. 73	9.14. 0. 0. 0	Initial Series
St. 8	9.14.10. 0. 0	Initial Series
St. 4	9.14. ?. ?. ?	Initial Series
St. 51	9.14.19. 5. 0	Initial Series
St. 52	9.15. 0. 0. 0	Initial Series
St. 53	9.15. 0. 0. 0	Period-Ending

St. 54	9.15. 0. 0. 0	Initial Series
St. 55	9.15. 0. 0. 0	Initial Series
St. 48	9.15. 0. 0. 0	Initial Series
St. 89	9.15. 0. 0.14	Initial Series
St. 26	9.15. 5. 0. 0	Initial Series
St. 25	9.15.10. 0. 0	Initial Series
St. 27	9.15.10. 0. 0	Initial Series
St. 59	9.15.10. 0. 0	Initial Series
St. 60	9.15.10. 0. 0	Initial Series
St. 62	9.16. 0. 0. 0	Period Ending
St. 57	9.17. 0. 0. 0	Initial Series
St. 58	9.17. 0. 0. 0	Initial Series
St. 80	9.18. 0. 0. 0	Initial Series
St. 67	9.18.10. 0. 0	Initial Series
St. 69	9.18.10. 0. 0	Initial Series
St. 15	9.19. 0. 0. 0	Period-Ending
St. 16	9.19. 0. 0. 0	Initial Series
St. 64	9.19. 0. 0.0?	Initial Series
St. 65	9.19.10. 0.0?	Style Dating
St. 39	9.'?. ?. ?. ?	Initial Series
St. 45	9.? 10. 0. 0	Initial Series
St. 66	9.18. 0. 0.0?	Style Dating
St. 17	10. 0. 0. 0.0?	Style Dating
St. 84	10. 3. ?. ?. ?	Style Dating
St. 91	10. 3. 0. 0.0?	Style Dating

While noting that the inhabitants of Calakmul had marked the ends of successive five-year (*hotunob*), ten-year (*lahuntunob*), and twenty-year (*katunob*) periods by dedicating dated stelae, Morley was struck by the fact that some period endings -- particularly those of ten- and twenty-year periods -- were commemorated by the erection of two, three, or four stelae. In one case, at the end of the fifteenth *katun* (9.15.0.0.0), in A.D. 731, seven monuments were carved and dedicated. Morley commented that "no other city ... displayed such consistent prodigality [*sic*] in the erection of its period markers as did Calakmul" (Morley 1933:200). Given the view prevalent in the 1930s that all stelae served as time-markers, Morley's statement is understandable. However, given the more recent genealogical and dynastic interpretations of Proskouriakoff, Berlin, Kelley, and others, nowadays we would be more inclined to interpret the simultaneous dedication of seven stelae in other ways (see section entitled Rulers at Calakmul).

THE MEDIUM

Unquestionably, the *stela* is the dominant medium for hieroglyphic inscriptions at Calakmul. This contrasts with the situation at Palenque (and a few other sites) where there are many inscriptions but very few stelae. At sites of the latter type, more extensive use is made of lintels, wall panels, altars, stairways, boulder sculptures, and sometimes "zoomorphs" for the display of hieroglyphic inscriptions. Thus, it is clear that for some sites the stela was deemed the appropriate medium for the display of texts, while at other sites different media were preferred. As we will see below, the *subject matter* of the inscriptions was *one* of the factors determining whether the stela (or some other medium) was selected as the form of display for permanent records.

Stelae -- in contrast to most lintels or wall slabs -- are often truly monumental pieces of stone sculpture, not infrequently portraying the ruler as greater than lifesize or even more than twice his actual height.   Additionally, stelae are freestanding "*outdoor*" or "public" displays often depicting a ruler on the front face and occasionally his wife on the back.   Often stelae are set up in lines at the base of a public building.   In contrast, lintels and wall slabs are usually much smaller, requiring one to read the inscription from close up.   (The Yaxchilán or Piedras Negras wall slabs or lintels would be examples).   Such wall slabs or lintels were not highly visible or accessible, sometimes occurring in the rear walls or doorways of dark rooms, unlike the more "public" stelae.   Unlike stelae, lintels and wall slabs often depict on a single surface scenes that involve two or more individuals (for example, see the Piedras Negras sculpture in Figure 21).   Stelae are often carved on three or four surfaces or sides, with one individual depicted on the front and another on the back.

21. Bat Jaguar of Yaxchilán holds an audience at Piedras Negras. (Lintel 3, Piedras Negras, Guatemala; photo courtesy of and with the permission of the University Museum, University of Pennsylvania, Philadelphia.)

Thus we might appropriately ask why did the rulers of sites such as Yaxchilán place many of their dynastic records in the dark interiors of structures, while the Calakmul rulers chose to display their dynastic records on lines of stelae in front of temples? Why were some sites' dynastic records more accessible to public view than those of other sites? The answer may lie in the subject matter.

Some of the subject matter of the Yaxchilán inscriptions (for example, texts recorded on some risers/treads and lintels incorporated into structures) differs from that on the stelae of sites such as Calakmul.

Unlike some of the Yaxchilán lintels, which show royal women performing rites associated with ancestor worship, such as ritual bloodletting, the Calakmul stelae portray royal women in formal poses (Marcus 1974b:92; 1976b: Chapter V). These stelae showing royal Calakmul women are often set up next to those depicting their husbands, such that each husband and wife can look at each other. What is probably significant here is that the lintels found in the secluded rooms of palaces and elite residences are more concerned with *rituals* (such as the taking of prisoners, bloodletting, the invocation of the spirit of an ancestor, and the apotheosis of deceased rulers; see

Figures 44 - 47) which might have been performed out of public view. Support for such a suggestion comes from a number of polychrome vessels and the Bonampak murals which show the elite involved in bloodletting rites that take place indoors. Often these bloodletting rites are associated with the birth of an heir, marriage, or the death of a ruler. Such scenes of "private" and indoor ritual activity appear to be absent from stelae at Calakmul. Furthermore, the Piedras Negras and Yaxchilán lintels often portray additional members of the royal family engaged in ritual activity; in contrast, members of the royal family other than wives seem to be missing from the Calakmul stelae.

Could this mean that texts on the stelae at Calakmul were limited to a discussion of the more "public" activities of the ruler, while the texts on lintels at sites such as Yaxchilán were concerned with the more "private" rituals carried out indoors by members of the ruling family? Did the *content* of the text dictate both the medium employed, and the location where it would be displayed? Our answer is a qualified "yes", in recognition of the fact that the pattern is not without exceptions.

At the very least, it would seem that the medium utilized for texts at different Maya sites could provide clues to the nature of the subject matter. In addition, we have seen that the location of the text (outdoor *versus* indoor; in front of a temple *versus* the doorway of a palace room) and its visibility to the public are other important clues.

PATTERNS IN THE CALAKMUL DATA

In the pages that follow we will discuss the context, content, and provenience of the Calakmul monuments with the goal of understanding the role of writing in the hands of the Maya ruler and his administrative elite (Marcus 1976a).

The Calakmul stelae portray greater than lifesize royal men and women. Some individuals measure two or three meters in height; these massive portrayals on freestanding multi-ton stones create very powerful images, particularly when set up in bilaterally-symmetrical lines in front of impressive temples and public buildings. Significantly, the elite residences identified at Calakmul, and the palaces that form part of the principal plaza groups (for example, Structure III), do *not* have stelae set up in front of them. The close relationship between temples and stelae at Calakmul seems to relate to the divine right to rule, which will be the subject of a later section of this preliminary report.

Of interest here and in future reports are the ways in which the function and content of monuments at Calakmul are similar to and different from those of other Maya sites. Were the lifespans of Calakmul rulers longer than those of most citizens? Was the length of rulers' reigns systematically different from site to site and might this reflect different patterns of succession to the throne? Were monuments at different sites set up *after* the ruler had acceded to the throne, *after* his marriage, or *after* the birth of an heir? Many of these questions have been answered partially as a result of detailed studies at several different sites. Each case study reveals the diversity and distribution of specific practices, but it also increases our knowledge of many similarities and general patterns shared by nearly all Maya centers. In both respects, the data from Calakmul will be important, enabling us to document still another case with its particular characteristics, and revealing patterns seen elsewhere at other centers. For example, at Calakmul there is evidence that at least two events -- marriage and accession to the throne -- served as catalysts for the carving of paired monuments that honor royal couples. The topic of the royal couple at Calakmul [and the evidence for *post-nuptial* accession to the throne and *post-nuptial* dedication of stelae] will be discussed later in this report and will be the subject of lengthier treatment in the next report on the Calakmul inscriptions.

Patterning in the Calakmul hieroglyphic data can be used to contribute information on at least two levels: intra-site and inter-site. The intra-site level includes information about the individual ruler and the royal couple, as well as dynastic data linking one reign to another. This information permits us to document the rise and fall of particular dynasties within a site. The inter-site level would comprise data of two kinds: intra-regional and inter-regional. Information on the intra-regional level reveals how each site is linked to its hinterland and to the dependencies in its regional hierarchy. Inter-regional data show how sites in one region are linked to sites in a different region. Ultimately, these data can be used to reconstruct the territorial organization of the southern Maya lowlands. Since the latter topic was discussed at length in earlier publications (Marcus 1973, 1974a, 1976b, 1983a), we will not do so here. However, in later sections of this report we will see the many levels on which the Calakmul data contribute to our understanding of the operation of the ancient Maya state in southern Campeche.

THE RULERS OF CALAKMUL

The Calakmul stelae can be divided into several series, much as Proskouriakoff (1960) did with the Piedras Negras stelae, and other epigraphers such as Berlin (1968a, 1977), Kelley (1962), and Jones (1977) have accomplished at other sites. The purpose of dividing the stelae into such series is to determine the number of rulers, the lengths of reigns, and the presence of gaps between reigns.

In working with the Calakmul inscriptions, it is clear that there is more than one way that the stelae can be divided into series. One approach -- chronologically ordering all dated stelae and integrating these stelae with other lines of evidence, such as epigraphic, architectural, and contextual -- yields evidence for at least ten Calakmul rulers. It also reveals at least one major gap in our reconstructed sequence (between the reigns of Ruler 1 and 2). Some alternative methods for ordering the Calakmul monuments (which I plan to treat at length in a future report) produce lists of more than ten rulers. However, for the purposes of this preliminary report, I will present only the former reconstruction, which yielded ten possible Calakmul rulers.

RULER 1

The first ruler for whom we have data is named in several clauses on Stela 43, a monument that was carved and dedicated in A.D. 514 (see Figure 22). This stela stands over three meters high and portrays Ruler 1 on the front in the style we associate with the Early Classic period (Proskouriakoff 1950: Figure 40a).

22. Clauses that include the names and titles of Ruler 1 at Calakmul (from Stela 43, A9-B10, D2-C3, C7-C8, and D12-D13).

This style is characterized by a somewhat cluttered or crowded appearance in which there is little open space; there is use of high, medium, and low relief, in addition to many details added by incising. Some might describe this style as "baroque" or "ornate" when contrasting it with the less cluttered appearance of Late Classic stelae. While Morley (1933:200-201) and Denison (1943:100) were both reluctant to accept the A.D. 514 date as contemporaneous, it is clear that the monument conforms stylistically to Early Classic conventions (see Proskouriakoff 1950:108-109), and fortunately the Initial Series date of 9.4.0.0.0 is clear. Indeed, the style of Stela 43 is similar to other Early Classic monuments, such as Stela 31 from Tikal and Stela 6 from Yaxhá.

Ruler 1 is shown in profile view with an elaborate headdress framing his face; he holds a ceremonial bar diagonally positioned in his left arm, and associated with him are two bound captive figures. This monument provides us with a lengthy text, also quite characteristic of the Early Classic period. The text is recorded on the sides of the monument, while the back is plain. Ruler 1 at Calakmul would have been a contemporary of "Jaguar Paw Skull 1", a ruler at Tikal (who may have ruled from A.D. 488 to 537).

Stela 43 is one of the very few at Calakmul where one could make a good case that the monument originally had been erected in a different location and was later reset. Today, it stands on the first terrace on the north side of Structure II (see Figure 3), in apparent association with monuments that were carved, dedicated, and erected nearly 200 years later (*circa* A.D. 700).

On the left side of Stela 43 there is a very clear Initial Series Introductory Glyph (at A1-B2), followed by a date of 9.4.0.0.0 (A3-A4), the day 13 Ahau (B4), and the month 18 Yax (A5); this corresponds to October 16, A.D. 514. A number of important clauses (particularly those on the right side) provide the name and titles of this important early ruler (see Figure 22). Associated with Ruler 1 are two important dates, roughly a year and a half apart that refer to events that took place approximately thirteen years before the stela was dedicated.

RULER 2

Two carved monuments (Stelae 28 and 29) were set up 109 years after Stela 43 was dedicated. This pair of monuments was placed on the north side of Structure V; they are the only two stelae in that location. (Structure V lies on the south side of what became the Central Plaza; see Figure 3). The two stelae stand next to each other, a man on one monument and a woman on the other, each facing the other (see Figure 23). From these two monuments, we learn something about Ruler 2 as well as his wife.

Ruler 2's wife is portrayed on Stela 28; her husband appears on Stela 29 (see Figure 24). The monuments share a number of important features. In addition to each figure's placement on the front face, each also is associated with a hieroglyphic panel that frames the face, and with additional hieroglyphic texts on the sides of the monument; the back of each stela is plain. In the L-shaped hieroglyphic panels that frame the royal pair's faces are texts that contain their names.

23. In A.D. 623, Stelae 29 (foreground) and 28 (background) were set up on the north side of Structure V to honor Ruler 2 and his wife.

24. The royal couple, Ruler 2 (at right, Stela 29) and his wife (at left, Stela 28), face each other.

Additionally, each figure stands atop a bound captive; the captives, in turn, face each other. Thus, in design and layout these two monuments were clearly carved as a mirror-image pair. Further evidence of this pairing is the fact that both monuments record the same dedicatory date of March 19, A. D. 623 [9.9.10.0.0 (2 Ahau 13 Pop)]; see Figures 25 and 26.

During the era in which Morley and Denison were studying the Calakmul monuments, no Maya archaeologist imagined that women were among those individuals portrayed. Every investigator of that period assumed that all figures were men -- either priests wearing long skirts (since priests in Yucatán during the Postclassic and early Colonial periods were known to have worn long gowns or robes), or warriors wearing short skirts or loincloths. Thus, it is not surprising that the description of the woman on Stela 28 includes a statement that she is a "figure facing right, clasping both hands on his breast" (Denison 1943:105). Prior to Proskouriakoff's work (1960, 1961b, 1963, and 1964), women simply were not identified in Classic Maya stelae.

25. Two views of the right side of Stela 29, showing the Initial Series Introductory Glyph followed by the date 9.9.10.0.0 2 Ahau 13 Pop, which corresponds to March 19, A.D. 623. The text goes on to discuss Ruler 2. (Photo at left was taken during the day, while the one at right was taken at night.)

26. Part of the text discussing events in the life of Ruler 2 (left side, Stela 29).

As we will see, this marital pair from A.D. 623 is the first of at least five royal couples depicted on Calakmul stelae. While some royal women are commemorated at other primary Maya centers, one rarely encounters as many *different* women honored as is the case at Calakmul, nor does one find so many women depicted as protagonists on their own stelae. The more frequent pattern at secondary and lower-order centers is one in which one (rarely two) royal Maya woman was commemorated on her own stelae -- usually because she was a woman from the royal dynasty at the regional capital (who had "married down" and thereby elevated the status of the dependent center's ruler). The more frequently-encountered pattern at capitals is that royal wives are portrayed on the backs of stelae with their husbands depicted on the front. Although this latter pattern is also known from Calakmul, it is clear that Calakmul was different: it was a major regional capital which provided both members of a royal marital pair with their own stela.

Stela 1, accompanied by an altar, was set up in front of Structure VIII. This monument may have been dedicated to Ruler 2, or to a ruler who intervened between Rulers 2 and 3.

RULER 3

Ruler 3 may be commemorated on more stelae than any other Calakmul ruler. He appears to have been portrayed on Stelae 9, 13, 32, 33, 34, 35, 36, and 37, dedicated between A.D. 657 and 672. His wife is also known from her portrayal on the back of Stela 9, and from the recording of her name in the main text itself (see Figure 27) and in a single line of text incorporated as a band near the bottom of her skirt (see Figures 58 and 59). She may also be portrayed on the back of another monument.

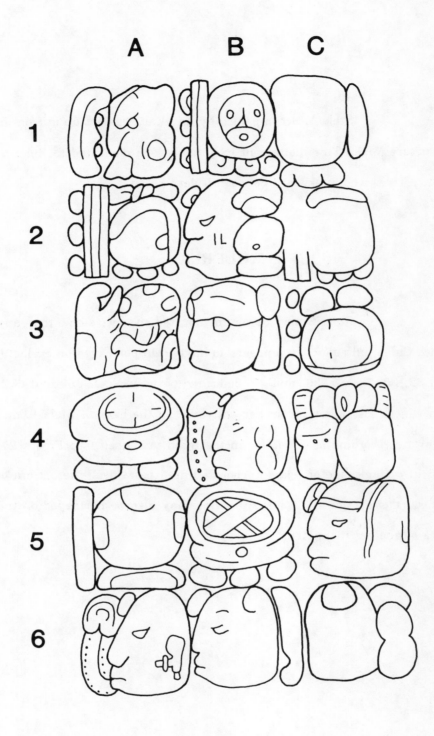

27. The wife of Ruler 3 is named in this glyph panel from the back of Stela 9. The Calendar Round date of 11 Ahau 18 Chen (at B1-A2) corresponds to August 21, A.D. 662, the same date that begins the text on the front of the same stela. On the front Ruler 3's name and portrait are given (see Ruppert and Denison 1943: Plate 48a and 48b).

To honor Ruler 3's reign, seven monuments were set up in association with Structure V and still others in front of Structure IVb, both localities in the Central Plaza.   The continued use of Structure V as a place to set up dynastic records may indicate that Ruler 3 was a relative of Ruler 2, or that he wished to legitimize his right to rule by linking himself to the latter's reign.

Near the base of the building on the south side of Structure V, six stelae were set up, three flanking either side of a centrally-placed altar.   Moving from west to east, we find Stela 37 (carved on all four sides); Stela 36 (carved on all four sides), with a date of A.D. 662 (9.11.10.0.0?); and Stela 35 with dates of A.D. 660 - 662 (9.11.8.10.8 and 9.11.10.0.0).   To the east of the altar are Stela 34 (with no clear date); Stela 33, set up in A.D. 657 (9.11.5.0.0 ?); and Stela 32 (carved on all four sides) with an apparent date of A.D. 672 (Initial Series date of 9.12.0.0.0).   Additionally, two apparently plain monuments (Stelae 30 and 31) were placed atop Structure V.

Two significant characteristics of the group of stelae on the south side of Structure V are (1) that the group was set up as an evenly-spaced line to either side of a centrally-placed plain altar, and (2) that the span of time covered by the dedicatory dates does not exceed 15 years (A.D. 657 - 672). This span apparently constitutes all or part of Ruler 3's reign.

Monuments set up to honor Ruler 3 were also erected in front of Structure IVb. Stela 9 was originally set up near the northwest corner of Structure IVb (it has been moved to the Campeche museum). This beautifully-carved stela records four dates --- 9.10.16.16.19 (3 Cauac 2 Ceh), 9.11.10.0.0 (11 Ahau 18 Chen), 9.11.18.3.0 [13 Ahau 18 (?) Yax, although it looks more like 13 Ahau 16 Yax], and 9.12.0.0.0 (10 Ahau 8 Yaxkin). Stela 13 was set up near Stela 9 and displays a date of A.D. 672 (an Initial Series date of 9.12.0.0.0). Given the Initial Series dates recorded on Stelae 9 and 13, it seems likely that Ruler 3 was honored by them as well.

RULER 4

Monuments erected to commemorate the reign of Ruler 4 include those associated with Structures XV, XVI, XVIII, and IX. All these structures are located outside the Central Plaza, the area that had been the focus of monuments honoring all previous rulers.

A line of five stelae honoring Ruler 4 was set up in front of Structure XV.   As we proceed from north to south along this important line of monuments, we see that each commemorates the ending of a five-year period and that all the *hotunob* are consecutive.

Table 2. Five-year period endings commemorated by Ruler 4 on stelae erected in front of Structure XV.

Stela Number	Long Count Date	Gregorian Date
75	9.12. 0. 0. 0	A. D. 672
76	9.12. 5. 0. 0	A. D. 677
77	9.12.10. 0. 0	A. D. 682
78	9.12.15. 0. 0	A. D. 687
79	9.13. 0. 0. 0	A. D. 692

The span of time represented by these stelae is approximately twenty years (from 9.12.0.0.0 to 9.13.0.0.0) and within that time span it appears that Ruler 4's reign falls.

Set up on the north side of Structure XVIII was Stela 86, with an Initial Series date of A.D. 672 (9.12.0.0.0), along with Stelae 85 and 87, whose dedicatory dates are not clear. Another date of A.D. 672 was recorded on Stela 74, and a date of A.D. 680 [9.12.8.9.9 ? (11 Muluc 17 Kankin)] appears on Stela 70. These last two stelae flank a line of monuments set up in front of Structure XVI. While Stelae 70, 74, 85, and 86 appear to honor Ruler 4, all the dedicatory dates recorded on the intervening stelae of this group [Nos. 73, 72 (with associated altar), and 71] mention the date A.D. 711 [9.14.0.0.0 (6 Ahau 13 Muan)], and therefore presumably were erected to honor Ruler 6. It appears that the original intent was that the stelae honoring Ruler 4 faced each other across the Southeast Court in the West Group.

Two additional stelae (Nos. 93 and 94) with Initial Series dates of A.D. 682 [9.12.10.0.0 (9 Ahau 18 Zotz)] were set up in association with Structure IX and probably also relate to Ruler 4.

RULER 5

Ruler 5's monuments began with the dedication of a pair of stelae set up toward the east side atop Structure VI. Ruler 5 is portrayed on Stela 24, while Stela 23 depicts his wife; both stelae bear the Initial Series date of A.D. 702 [9.13.10.0.0 (7 Ahau 3 Cumhu)]. A plain round altar was placed between this marital pair.

Just like the marital pair consisting of Ruler 2 and his wife, these stelae share a number of features pointing to their having been carved as a pair and dedicated simultaneously. Like Ruler 2 and his wife, Ruler 5 and his wife stand on bound captives, are displayed on the front face of their stelae, and are accompanied by texts on both sides, with the back of the monuments left plain.

A case can be made that Structure VI, the stelae commemorating the marital pair, and the altar set between them were all dedicated on January 24, A.D. 702. Ruler 5 was also honored by the dedication of three stelae in association with Structure II. These stelae -- Nos. 38, 40, and 41 -- also record the *katun* period ending in A.D. 702.

RULER 6

Four stelae were set up in association with Structures XVI and IVa to honor Ruler 6. As indicated above, Stelae 71, 72, and 73 were set up in A.D. 711 in association with Structure XVI; Stela 8 (see Figure 28) was set up in A.D. 721 apparently in association with the southwest corner of Structure IVa.

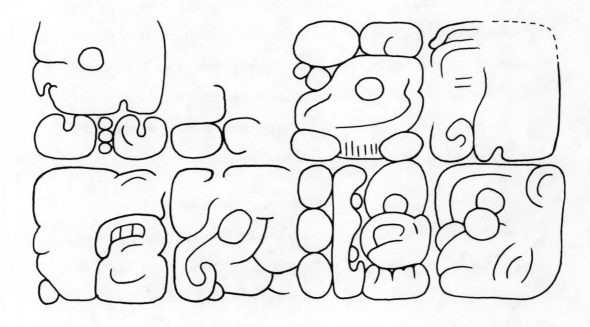

28. Hieroglyphic passage from Stela 8, set up on October 11, A.D. 721 to honor Ruler 6 and his wife. (Both lines are from the left side; the top line runs from C7 to D8, the bottom line from C9 to D10).

RULER 7

The construction of Structure I apparently took place during the reign of Ruler 7, who is honored by a series of monuments set up in association with the building. Stela 89, placed at the summit of Structure I, records a date of September 3, A.D. 731 (9.15.0.0.14) [see Figure 29]. A series of additional monuments (Stelae 48, 51, 52, 53, 54, and 55) were set up at the base of the structure (see Figures 30-32). The woman portrayed on Stela 54 may be the wife of Ruler 7.

29. Stela 89, erected on the top of Structure I, honors Ruler 7. On a fragment left behind by looters (photo, at top) we can see what remains of part of the text [the intact left side was published by Morley (1933:201) and Ruppert and Denison (1943: Plate 53c)]. Shown in the drawing below are the A7-B7 and A8-B8 glyph blocks, which may include another name (or title) of Ruler 7.

30. Stela 51, called by Morley (1933:200) "the most beautiful monument at Calakmul", honors Ruler 7. In contrast to most Calakmul stelae, this was found in excellent condition, because it had fallen face down. (Photo courtesy of Tatiana Proskouriakoff, taken by the Carnegie Institution of Washington in the 1930s.)

31. Stela 51. This 1983 photo shows how looters cut the stela into square blocks for transport. Ruler 7's monument now resides in the Museo Nacional de Antropología in Mexico City.

32. Ruler 7's name clause from Stela 51, beginning with an event that occurred on the Calendar Round date of 10 Ahau 13 Chen.

Further, it appears that Stela 52 and Stela 54 were carved as a pair, because the ruler on Stela 52 is the only individual that faces the woman, and they share other specific features that are discussed under the heading of royal marital pairs.

RULER 8

Ruler 8's monuments were set up on the west side of Structure VI and the east side of Structure XIV; the two sets of stelae face each other across an open area. The first monument placed on the west side of Structure VI was Stela 26 [9.15.5.0.0 (10 Ahau 8 Chen)]; it was centrally located and associated with a plain, round altar. Approximately five years later, in A.D. 741 (9.15.10.0.0), Stelae 25 and 27 were set up to either side of the first stela and altar. At that same time, two other stelae (Nos. 59 and 60) were placed on the east side of Structure XIV. Finally, ten years later (A.D. 751), Stela 62 was set up on the west side of Structure XIV.

The fact that Ruler 8 places his monuments in association with Structure VI -- a building possibly constructed and renovated by Ruler 5 -- may indicate that Ruler 8 wished to link himself to that earlier reign. Whether or not he was related biologically to the earlier ruler is unclear.

RULER 9

The next series of monuments, set up at the West Group, was designed to honor Ruler 9. On the east side of Structure XIII, at least two monuments (Stelae 57 and 58) were erected with dates of A.D. 771 [9.17.0.0.0 (13 Ahau 18 Cumhu)]. On the north side of Structure XVII (the building delimiting the southern end of the Southeast Court), Stela 80 was erected in A.D. 790 [9.18.0.0.0 (11 Ahau 18 Mac)]. Ten years later, in A.D. 800, three more monuments (Stelae 67, 68, and 69) were set up to the southwest of the sculptured outcrop that depicts seven bound captives. On the cover of this report is one of these nude figures (redrawn from Eric von Euw's original sketch).

RULER 10

Ruler 10's monuments were placed in the Central Plaza and the West Group. In A.D. 810 [9.19.0.0.0 (9 Ahau 18 Mol)] Stelae 15 and 16 were erected in front of Structure IVb in the Central Plaza and their placement there links Ruler 10 to one of the earlier Calakmul rulers, Ruler 3. Stelae 63, 64, and 65, on the other hand, were placed to the north of Structure X, in the North Court of the West Group. Additional monuments with eroded Initial Series dates may also honor Ruler 10 or a still later ruler.

TEMPLES AND ASSOCIATED STELAE THAT COMPRISE PLAZA GROUPS

Just as Proskouriakoff (1960) divided the stelae at Piedras Negras into a chronologically-ordered sequence, we can divide Calakmul's stelae into chronologically-ordered clusters on the basis of their dedicatory dates and other epigraphic data. Using these stelae and their associations with specific structures, we can suggest a tentative chronological order for the structures as well.

In most cases, these clusters of stelae appear to constitute dynastic records covering part or all of a ruler's reign; occasionally, they may span a longer period of time. However, we can conclude that nearly all of the lines of stelae set up in front of individual structures appear to span reigns. In fact, in only one case does the span between the earliest date and the latest date clearly exceed that of a normal human lifetime -- specifically, in the case of the stelae set up on the west side of Structure IVb. And in that case, it appears that a later ruler decided to associate his stelae with those of a much earlier ruler who may have been one of his ancestors.

If we assume that each ruler actually *dedicated* the individual buildings (or enlargements or modifications on an extant structure) with which his stelae are associated, we have a unique opportunity at Calakmul. The precise dating provided by the stelae might allow us to present a tentative chronology for the order in which certain buildings were dedicated at Calakmul (see Figures 33-42 following Table 3). These dates and structures are given in the table on the next page.

Table 3. Stelae Dates and Associated Structures.

Long Count Dates	Associated Structure
9.9.10.0.0	Str. V (north side)
9.10.?.?.5	Structure VIII
9.11.5.0.0-9.12.0.0.0	Str. V (south side)
9.12.0.0.0	Str. IVb
9.12.0.0.0-9.13.0.0.0	Str. XV, XVI, XVIII, IX
9.13.10.0.0	Str. VI, II
9.14.0.0.0	Str. XVI
9.14.10.0.0	Str. IVa
9.15.0.0.0	Str. I
9.15.5.0.0-9.15.10.0.0	Str. VI (west side)
9.15.10.0.0	Str. XIV (east side)
9.17.0.0.0	Str. XIII
9.18.0.0.0	Str. XVII
9.19.0.0.0	Str. IVb, X

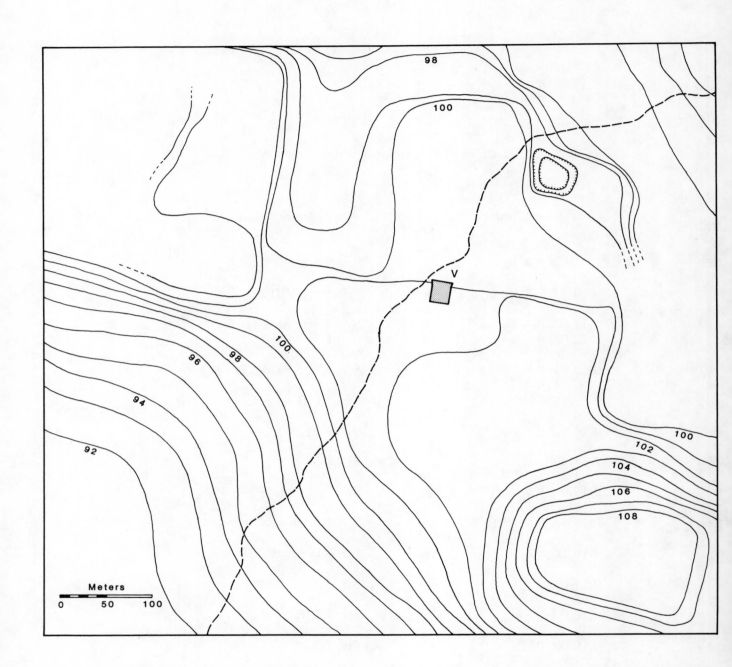

33. Structure V, dedicated around A.D. 623, shaded and superimposed on a contour map of Calakmul; this was the oldest building associated with dated stelae. (In Figures 33-42, contour interval is one meter; the dashed line indicates the trail to Central Buenfil which lies to the northeast.)

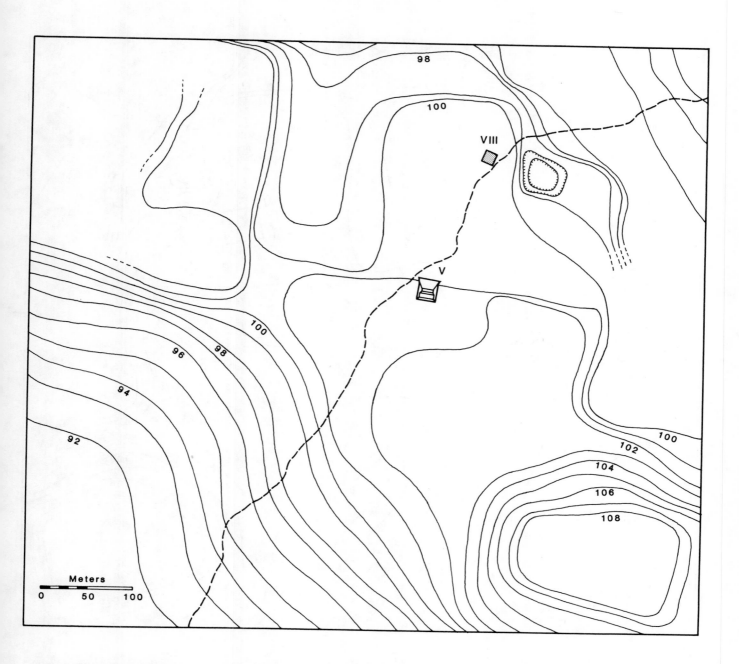

34. Structure VIII, dedicated around A.D. 633, shaded and superimposed on a contour map of Calakmul. (In Figures 34-42, previously dedicated buildings are left unshaded.)

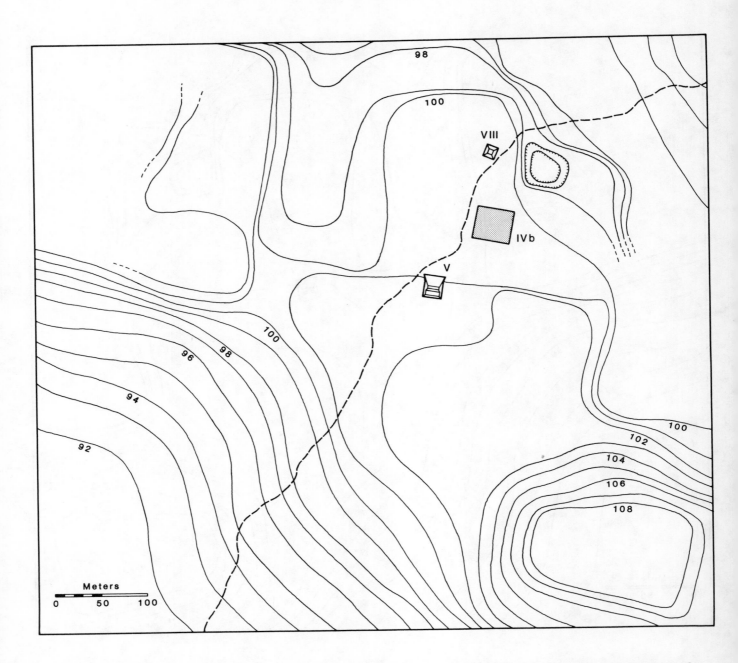

35. Structure IVb, dedicated around A.D. 672, shaded and superimposed on a contour map of Calakmul. (In Figures 34-42, previously dedicated buildings are left unshaded.)

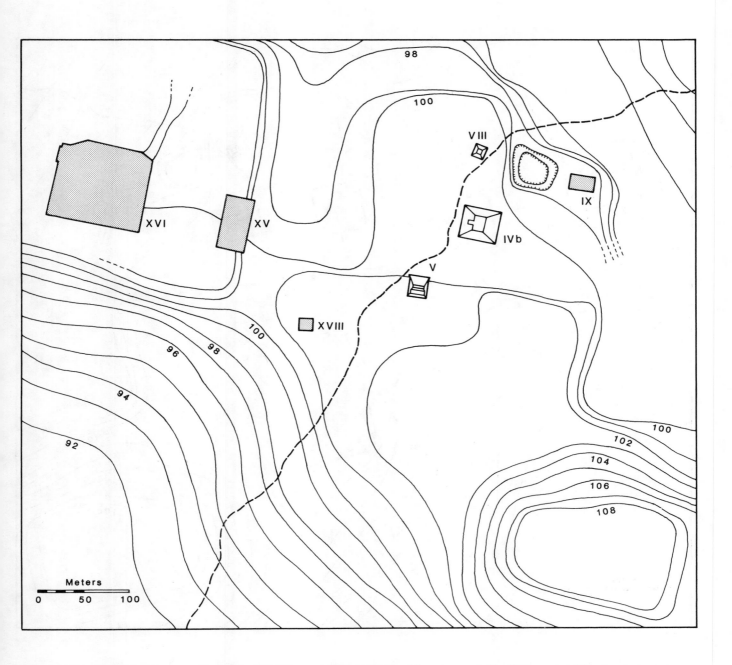

36. Four structures --XVI, XV, XVIII, and IX--dedicated between A.D. 672 and 682, shaded and superimposed on a contour map of Calakmul. (In Figures 34-42, previously dedicated buildings are left unshaded.)

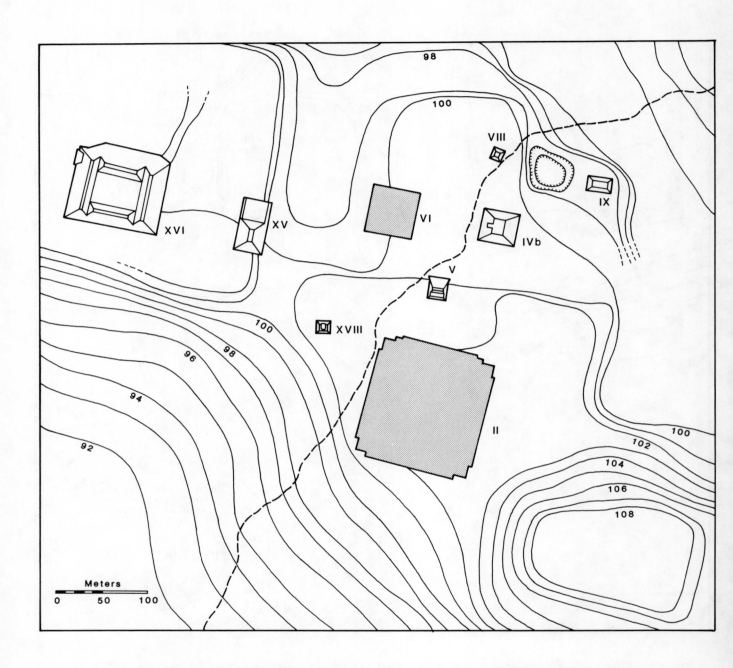

37. Structures II and VI, dedicated around A.D. 702, shaded and superimposed on a contour map of Calakmul. (In Figures 34-42, previously dedicated buildings are left unshaded.)

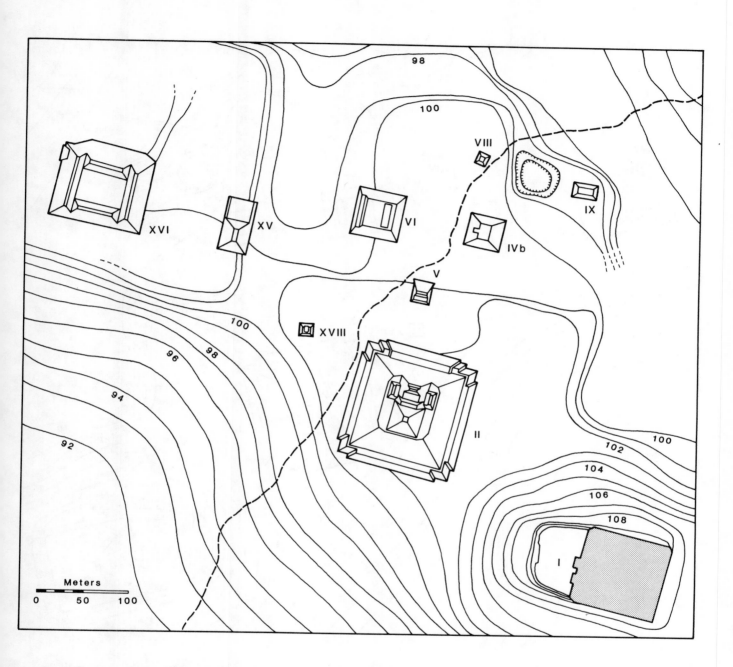

38. Structure I, dedicated around A.D. 731, shaded and superimposed on a contour map of Calakmul. (In Figures 34-42, previously dedicated buildings are left unshaded.)

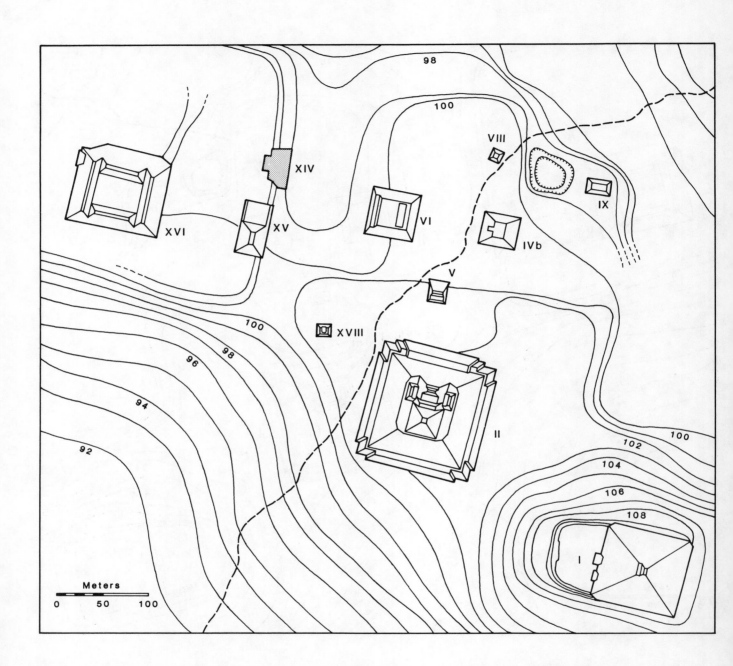

39. Structure XIV, dedicated between A.D. 741 and 751, shaded and superimposed on a contour map of Calakmul. (In Figures 34-42, previously dedicated buildings are left unshaded.)

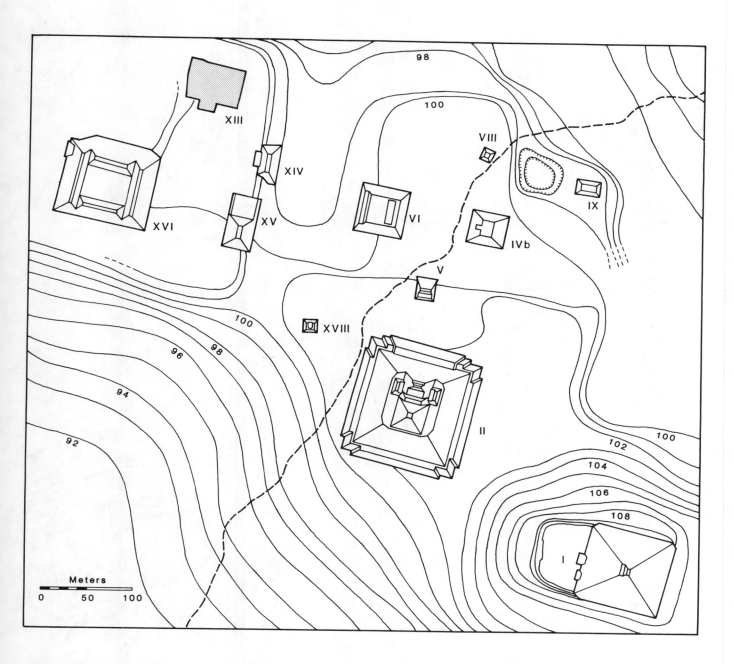

40. Structure XIII, dedicated around A.D. 771, shaded and superimposed on a contour map of Calakmul. (Previously dedicated buildings are left unshaded.)

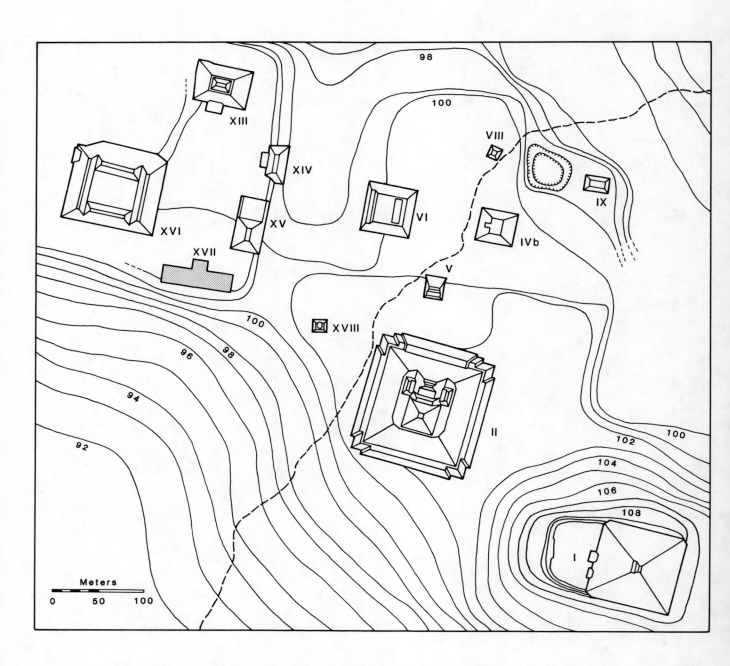

41. Structure XVII, dedicated around A.D. 790, shaded and superimposed on a contour map of Calakmul. (Previously dedicated buildings are left unshaded.)

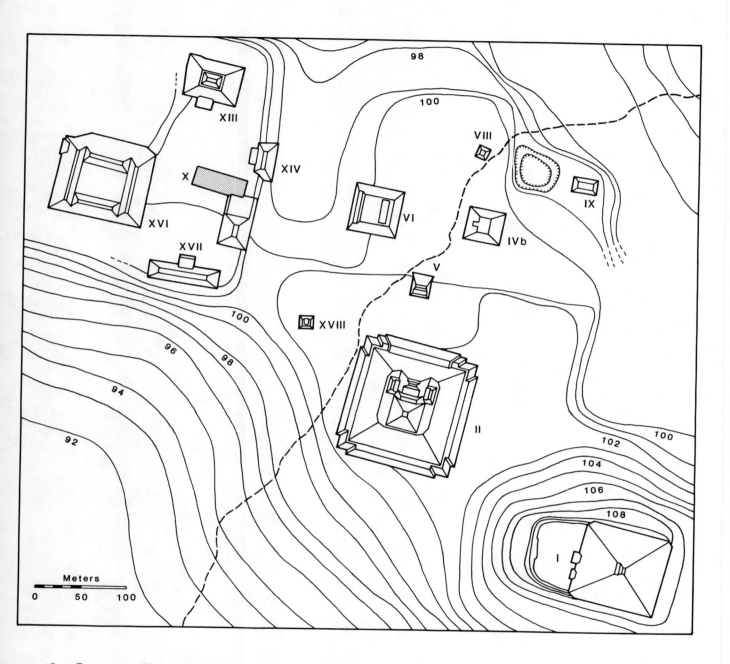

42. Structure X, dedicated around A.D. 810, shaded and superimposed on a contour map of Calakmul. This structure divided a large court into two smaller ones, the North Court and the Southeast Court. (Previously dedicated buildings are left unshaded.)

CHRONOLOGICAL SEQUENCE OF STELAE
AND THEIR CONTEXT

The next task is to link individual reigns with the dedication of stelae and temples. Although alternative reconstructions were carefully considered, I present here the reconstruction supported by the most lines of evidence. Table 4 (see next page) provides in chronological order the reigns of the ten Calakmul rulers, their stelae, and associated structures.

Table 4. Linking The Reigns of Ten Calakmul Rulers to Their Public Buildings.

Stela Date	Associated Structure	Stela Number	Possible Ruler #
A.D. 514	Reset on Str. II	43	1
A.D. 623	Str. V (N side)	28, 29	2
A.D. 633?	Str. VIII	1	2a?
A.D. 648-672	Str. IVb	9, 13	
A.D. 657-672	Str. V (S side)	30- 37	3
A.D. 672	Str. XVIII	86	
A.D. 672-680	Str. XVI	74, 70	4
A.D. 682	Str. IX	93, 94	
A.D. 672-692	Str. XV (W side)	75-79	
A.D. 702	Str. VI	23, 24, altar	
A.D. 702	Str. II	38, 40, 41	5

A.D. 711	Str. XVI	71, 72, 73	
A.D. 721	Str. IVa	8	6
A.D. 731	Str. I	48, 51-55, 89	7
A.D. 736-41	Str. VI (W side)	26, 25, 27	
A.D. 741	Str. XIV	59, 60, 62	8
A.D. 771	Str. XIII(East)	57, 58	
A.D. 790	Str. XVII	80	9
A.D. 800	Sculptured Outcrop	67, 69	
A.D. 810	Str. IVb	15, 16, 17	10
A.D. 810	Str. X	64, 65	

Now we might comment briefly on a few of the patterns revealed in these data. First, the Central Plaza seems to have been the focus for the earliest rulers of Calakmul, while most of the later rulers preferred the West Group or the Southeast Group for the placement of their stelae. Second, within the Central Plaza it appears that Structure V was the first building dedicated, followed by

Structures VIII and IVb. Later, outside the Central Plaza, Structures XVIII, XVI, IX, and XV were inaugurated. Finally, Structures VI, II, I, XIV, XIII, XVII, and X were completed and stelae were set up in association with them (see Figures 33-42).

THE CALAKMUL REALM

Like the ancient Maya residing in other major cities of Honduras, Guatemala, Belize, Tabasco, and Quintana Roo, the Maya of Campeche were active participants in a political, administrative, and ritual system that linked the elite of different regions. Within each major region there was a primary administrative center that headed the regional hierarchy. Calakmul was one of these primary centers, administering a large area within southern Campeche. Calakmul was surrounded by a hexagonal wheel of secondary administrative centers, some falling within the modern Mexican state of Campeche, while others lay in the northwestern corner of the Guatemalan Department of Petén (see Figures 2 and 43).

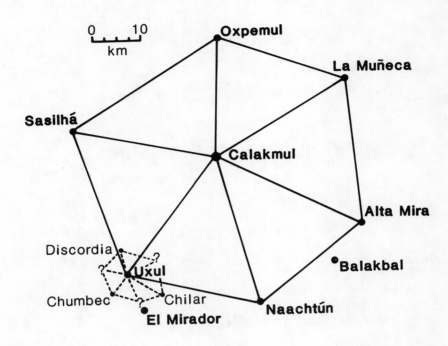

43. The site of Calakmul, linked by straight lines to the dependencies that were part of its Late Classic realm. Possible tertiary sites around Uxul are also shown.

An unanswered question is whether or not the large site of El Mirador ever formed part of Calakmul's realm, or whether it reached its peak too early to be involved. If El Mirador's heyday occurred during the Late or Terminal Preclassic period, as Matheny (1980) and Demarest (1984) believe, we will need to determine whether another city became the dominant local center during the Early Classic; alternatively, it might be that El Mirador and Calakmul co-existed for a time as co-dominant sites during the Early Classic. At any rate, it appears that Calakmul eventually gained the upper hand in this area, becoming the dominant regional center during the Late Classic period. It may therefore be that as El Mirador's power waned, Calakmul's waxed. To judge from its dated stelae, Calakmul's heyday as primary center spanned the Late Classic period -- A.D. 600-850 -- but it had certainly been occupied during the Early Classic, and perhaps even earlier.

The patterns revealed by the stelae erected at Calakmul's dependencies reveal some surprising and important patterns. These dependencies included (moving clockwise from the north) Oxpemul, La Muñeca, Alta Mira, Balakbal(?), Naachtún, Uxul, and Sasilhá (see Figure 43). Many of these sites have impressive numbers of monuments, but few of their stelae and altars are in good condition; this weathering makes it difficult to read the Initial Series dates, and even more difficult to extract all the non-calendric data that we would like. The total number of monuments known so far for the "realm" (Calakmul plus its major dependencies) exceeds 250.

One of the surprising patterns revealed in the data from Calakmul's dependencies is the span of dated monuments at each site.

Table 5. Calakmul's Dependencies and the Time Span of Their
Monuments

Site	Number of Monuments	Span of Dates
Balakbal	5	[8.18.9.17.18- ?]
Naachtún	45	[9.3.10.0.0-9.16.10. 0.0]
Uxul	21	[9.10.10.0.0 -9.12.0. 0.0]
Oxpemul	19	[9.15.0.0.0 -10.0. 0. 0.0]
La Muñeca	19	[9.13.0.0.0 -10.3. 0. 0.0]
Alta Mira	19	[? - ?]

Now we will look briefly at some of these dependencies
and their carved monuments.

BALAKBAL

Prior to the erection of the first stela at Calakmul,
Balakbal set up Stela 5 [Initial Series date of 8.18.9.17.18 (9 Etznab
16 Pop)]. This monument was dedicated during Cycle (or Baktun) 8

and is contemporaneous with stelae erected at Uaxactún, Tikal, and Uolantún, and perhaps with a tomb mural at Río Azul, all located in the Department of Petén, Guatemala. Although very little is known about Balakbal, the earliness of this Initial Series date suggests that the site was commemorating its elite even before such practices had begun at Calakmul.

Another practice which appears earlier at Balakbal is the association of stelae with temples; in fact, three of the five Balakbal stelae were found in temples. Stelae 2 and 3 were both found in the back of Structure V, the former in the northwest corner and the latter in the southwest. The Cycle 8 stela -- Stela 5 -- was painted red and buried near the center of the back wall of another temple (Structure XII).

NAACHTÚN

Stela 23, another monument that may predate Calakmul's earliest stela, was set up at Naachtún in A.D. 504 [its date is 9.3.10.0.0, according to Denison (1943:153), although Morley (1938, Volume III:326-328) placed it at 9.4.10.0.0 (12 Ahau 8 Mol), some ten years later than Calakmul's first stela]. Naachtún continued to erect early monuments between A.D. 534 and 564 (Stela 3 in 9.5.0.0.0 and Stela 5 in 9.6.10.0.0 ?). These last two Naachtún monuments would postdate the only known stela erected for Ruler 1 at Calakmul (A.D. 514).

Stela 1 (9.9.10.0.0) and Stela 2 (9.10.10.0.0) were erected in association with Structure XXV at Naachtún and commemorate periods ending in A.D. 623 and 642, respectively. These dates are contemporaneous with monuments dedicated to Calakmul Rulers 2 and 3.

Naachtún's Stela 21, located in the northwest corner of Structure V in Group C, appears to portray a royal woman. Additionally, a woman is mentioned in the inscription on the right side of Stela 10; she appears to be a different woman from that portrayed on Stela 21. The importance of women at secondary centers like Naachtún is not unexpected, for the reasons given in other sections of this report (e.g., p. 78).

Between A.D. 720 (?) and A.D. 761, at least four more stelae were carved at Naachtún (Stelae 15, 9, 8, and 10). These monuments would probably fall within the reigns of Calakmul Rulers 7 and 8, who reigned during the period A.D. 731 - A.D. 761. The more securely-dated monuments are Stela 9 at 9.15.0.0.0, Stela 8 at 9.16.0.0.0, and Stela 10 at 9.16.10.0.0. Stelae 9 and 8 were set up in association with Structure XIX and may be but two of the monuments dedicated to one important Naachtún ruler.

UXUL

During the reigns of Calakmul Rulers 2 and 3, important monuments were also set up at Uxul. All the dates that we have been able to read on Uxul's monuments fall within the period from A.D. 623 to 672. In other words, our sample of dated monuments at Uxul corresponds closely to the span of time covered by the monuments dedicated to just those two Calakmul rulers.

Just south of Structure II at Uxul, Stela 2 was erected. The figure on the front of Stela 2 appears to be a royal woman, and she is looking at the male figure on the front of Stela 3, which was set up to the south of Structure III. This possible marital pair may represent the marriage of a Calakmul woman to a local Uxul lord. The associated dedicatory date on both stelae is eroded but one still can see

9. 9. ?. ?. ? . In addition, Altar 2, placed on the south side of Structure VI, records three Initial Series dates that may be related to events in the life of this same marital couple. Those dates are 9.9.9.9.18 (9 Etznab 16 Zac), 9.10.9.17.0 (6 Ahau 18 Mac), and 9.10.10.0.0 (13 Ahau 18 Kankin). This Uxul couple was contemporaneous with Calakmul Ruler 2 and his wife.

A promising line of research for the future might include the excavation of those structures at Uxul that are associated with dated stelae erected during the reigns of specific Calakmul rulers. Some questions that might be partially answerable with such excavation data (assuming more epigraphic information is included in the tombs and caches in those structures) are as follows: Did a sister of Calakmul Ruler 2 marry a lord of Uxul (a practice we have seen used to link Tikal to Naranjo, and Yaxchilán to Bonampak)? If so, did monuments at Uxul continue to be dedicated to that woman's offspring during the reign of Calakmul Ruler 3? Were Structures II and III at Uxul built following the marriage of a Calakmul woman with an Uxul lord? Such research might secure more information on the interrelationships of Calakmul and Uxul, on the one hand, and Uxul and other centers, on the other.

At a later date, other stelae at Uxul were carved with the Initial Series dates of 9.11.10.0.0 (Stelae 12 and 13) and 9.12.0.0.0 (Stela 6), dates that would fall within the reign of Calakmul Ruler 3. Significantly, Stelae 12 and 13 were paired, erected on opposite sides of the main stairway halfway up the east side of Structure XI. These two individuals face each other conforming to a pattern we have seen elsewhere (especially at the regional capital, Calakmul). Stela 13 appears to depict a man, while Stela 12 may prove to be a woman; hence we may have another marital pair.

OXPEMUL

All nineteen stelae at Oxpemul were carved, and every stela was accompanied by an altar; however, fifty per cent of the altars were plain. The Oxpemul dates span the reigns of Calakmul Rulers 7 - 10.

Table 6.   Long Count Dates Reported from Oxpemul.

Stela	*Date*
Stela 12	9.15.0.0.0
Stela 17	9.15.0.0.0
Stela 11	9.15.10.0.0
Stela 13	9.15.10.0.0
Stela 9	9.16.0.0.0
Stela 18	9.16.5.0.0
Stela 19	9.16.5.0.0
Stela 2	9.17.0.0.0
Stela 4	9.17.0.0.0
	GAP
Stela 7	10.0.0.0.0

LA MUÑECA (XAMANTÚN)

While the dates of the two sites' monuments overlap, some of La Muñeca's monuments were set up after Calakmul had ceased to erect stelae. For example, Stela 1 at La Muñeca bears a date of A.D. 889 (10.3.0.0.0). In fact, in contrast with the lengthy span of dated monuments at Calakmul, all but one of La Muñeca's monuments were set up between A.D. 780 and 889. Denison (1943:123) noted that La Muñeca's first stela was erected 80 years after Calakmul's first, and its last stela was erected 80 years after Calakmul's last Initial Series date had been recorded. However, there are some Calakmul stelae whose dates are illegible and which stylistically could date to early Cycle 10, so the final word has not been stated on the two sites' relationship nor when Calakmul ceased to carve monuments.

ALTA MIRA

Unfortunately, none of the nineteen monuments at Alta Mira was in sufficiently good condition to permit Morley or Denison to read any Initial Series dates. However, both authors noted a number of long inscriptions, all the while lamenting the fact that they consisted of "non-calendrical texts". Some of the Alta Mira monuments are exceedingly tall; for example, Stela 10 is 5.65 meters high while Stela 12 measures 5.36 meters. The site will provide a challenge to future epigraphers.

MAINTAINING THE DIVINE RIGHT TO RULE

There were several ways in which Maya rulers legitimized their right to rule; in this preliminary report we will touch on just a few. One method was to link themselves to supernatural beings and to powerful natural forces which were considered not only animate but also sacred (Marcus 1978, 1983a). These forces were viewed as having the qualities that were appropriate for the Maya elite.

Another method by which the divine right to rule was maintained was through permanent written records linking contemporary rulers to royal ancestors, some of whom had been earlier rulers. Thus the living ruler attempted to mediate between the ruled, on the one hand, and his divine royal ancestors and a series of associated supernaturals, on the other. To these ends, permanent records were kept and both iconography and hieroglyphic writing were employed to establish the rulers' links to the supernatural and to their royal ancestors.   Examples of iconography that aided in these ends include various ritual scenes with their related hieroglyphic passages (Figures 44-47). For example, certain bloodletting rites performed on behalf of the deceased ruler by his widow served to link him to his ancestors as well as his offspring (Marcus 1978:185-186).

The placement of these permanent written records was important in the establishment of the divine right to rule. Stelae at Calakmul were clearly set up in association with temples (*kuna -- ku*, "sacred"; *na*, "house"). These monuments were often placed in lines that were bilaterally symmetrical, immediately in front of the pyramidal base that supported a temple. Such architectural structures have been likened to the mountains that housed ancestral spirits for the highland Maya (Vogt 1964a:37-38, 1964b:390).

44. Yaxchilán's Lintel 25, showing at lower right a kneeling woman holding a vessel with a bloodletter (a stingray spine?), blood-spattered papers, and the bloodletting hieroglyph itself. At left is a huge double-headed serpent above a vessel containing blood-spattered papers and a cord. In the open mouth of the serpent is the bust of a deceased ruler, shown holding a shield in his left hand and a spear in his right. Encircled by part of the serpent's body is a hieroglyphic panel that begins with the hieroglyph "deceased" (T-93.672:142). This text is read from right to left, the reverse of standard reading order. This "serpent rite" may have been related to the accession events taking place on the same day. This lintel was removed from the central doorway of Structure 23. The sculptured area measures 1.18 x .74 meters. (Courtesy of and with the permission of the British Museum, London.)

45.   Yaxchilán's Lintel 24 shows a woman (at right) passing through her tongue a thorny cord which leads to a basket with blood-spattered papers. The ruler, Shield Jaguar, stands with a staff held over her head. The hieroglyph for bloodletting is given in the panel behind his right hand, as are the name and title of the woman performing the bloodletting rite. This lintel was removed from the southeast doorway of Structure 23. The sculptured area measures 1.04 x 0.74 meters. (Courtesy of and with the permission of the British Museum, London.)

46. Yaxchilán's Lintel 17 shows a woman (at left) who passes through her tongue a cord leading to a vessel filled with blood-spattered papers. At right is Bird Jaguar, who reigned for sixteen years beginning in A.D. 752. The name of the woman (Jaguar Ix) is given in the hieroglyphic band at the bottom, while Bird Jaguar's name appears in the panel in front of his face. This bloodletting rite seems to be related to the birth of an heir, named Shield Jaguar II, who will succeed Bird Jaguar (Proskouriakoff 1963, 1964). The sculptured area is only 64 x 60 centimeters, and must be viewed up close to be comprehended. This lintel came from the northwest doorway of the central room of Structure 21; it was removed by A. P. Maudslay and deposited in the British Museum in 1883. (Courtesy of and with the permission of the British Museum, London.)

47. Yaxchilán's Lintel 15 shows a woman invoking the spirit of a dead ancestor. At right, she holds a basket containing a bloodletter (stingray spine?), blood-spattered papers, and the cord which she had used to pass through a fleshy organ (probably her tongue). At left, ascending from a vessel filled with blood-spattered papers, is a serpent in whose mouth is the face of the deceased. This lintel's sculptured area measures 80 x 67 centimeters. This monument was removed from the southeast doorway of the central chamber of Structure 21. (Courtesy of and with the permission of the British Museum, London.)

It has been suggested that the lowland Maya, lacking mountains in their natural environment, used temple pyramids as homologous counterparts. If the Classic Maya elite believed that their royal ancestors were descended from supernaturals that lived within pyramids, such a location would be an appropriate place for the burial of a ruler. Further, the Maya wished to link those rulers with the most sacred and unchanging structures they built; the top of such a pyramidal base would be an appropriate location for a temple. In fact, M. D. Coe (1956:393) has used the term "funerary temple" to describe the function of the temple-pyramid, concluding that "it was raised to house the tomb of an important personage" (*Ibid.*:392).

Both the placement of the stelae in front of temple-pyramids and the monuments' iconographic and hieroglyphic content reinforce the lack of separation between sacred and secular power in the Maya state. The most famous case of a royal tomb built prior to the construction of the pyramidal substructure and temple above is that of Palenque (Ruz 1954, 1958a, 1958b, 1958c, and 1958d).

At Calakmul excavations below the floor of the temple designated Structure VII revealed a funerary crypt with vaulted roof containing a 25 to 30-year-old male with approximately 2000 pieces of jade (including a mosaic mask, ring, plaques, and beads), flint knives and obsidian bloodletters, vessels, and a lip plug inscribed with a short text (Domínguez C. 1986, Gallegos G. 1985); however, unlike the Palenque tomb, this one was apparently built *after* the pyramid and temple. There is little doubt that the individuals buried in tombs below temples are royalty and that such placement links them to the sacred. Those buried directly below the floor of a palace (Structure III) at Calakmul may be members of the lesser nobility, who are evidently not worthy of the treatment afforded royalty, such as the construction of a vaulted roofed chamber, the placement of numerous jade offerings in the tomb, and the inclusion of objects inscribed with hieroglyphic inscriptions that record the name of the deceased. The carving of the deceased's name serves as a permanent memorial to him, preventing him from being forgotten as were the names of lesser nobility and the commoners.

At Calakmul, Maya rulers are often portrayed on stelae as larger-than-life individuals, wearing elaborate headdresses, carrying staffs of office, standing on scantily-clad captives, and accompanied by special paraphernalia used exclusively by royalty. Thus wrapped in the sanctity of the temple, the political and economic ends of the Maya state could be achieved.

ROYAL MARITAL PAIRS AT CALAKMUL

There are five probable royal couples depicted on the Calakmul stelae. One other pair of monuments dedicated in A.D. 692 will be discussed here since it has been suggested that it is from Calakmul; others suggest it was looted from El Perú or a third unknown site. We will deal with these six marital pairs in cursory fashion here, reserving the lengthier treatment they deserve for our next report. In Table 7 (see next page) the dates and building associations of the stelae depicting royal couples are given.

Table 7. Possible Royal Couples at Calakmul

Date	Female	Male	Building
A.D. 623	Stela 28	Stela 29	N. side, Str. V
A.D. 642-652?	Stela 88(B)*	Stela 88	S. side, Str.XIII
A.D. 662	Stela 9(B)*	Stela 9	W. Side, Str. IV
A.D. 692	Stela I#	Stela II#	Cleveland Kimbell#
A.D. 702	Stela 23	Stela 24	E. side, Str. VI
A.D. 731	Stela 54	Stela 52	W. side, Str. I

*(B) indicates the *back* of the stela.

#A royal woman is portrayed on Stela I which now resides in the Cleveland Museum of Art, Cleveland, Ohio (Miller 1974; Marcus 1976, frontispiece); her husband is shown on Stela II, presently housed at the Kimbell Art Museum, Fort Worth, Texas [see Figures 49 and 50]. These two monuments lack provenience, but are included here because Miller (1974) has suggested they were originally from Calakmul and because they share many stylistic attributes with the five Calakmul royal couples listed above. (Other scholars have suggested other proveniences, including El Perú.) Therefore, for comparative purposes and for the sake of completeness they will be discussed briefly in this report. The emblem glyphs in the texts will be discussed under the heading of the same name.

THE A.D. 623 COUPLE

Stelae 28 and 29 were carved as a pair (see Figure 48). Both display the same dedicatory date [9.9.10.0.0 (2 Ahau 13 Pop)] and were carved on three sides, with the back left plain. These stelae are nearly three meters high and are still standing on the north side of Structure V (see Figure 23). No other stelae were set up on the north side of this structure.

The two monuments show the marital pair facing each other. Both stand on crouching captives that occupy the lower register. The woman on Stela 28 holds both clenched hands to her chest, apparently holding a two-headed ceremonial serpent bar. Her name panel is L-shaped and frames her face and headdress. The man on Stela 29 lets his arms hang beside him; a dwarf-like figure appears below his right hand. The male ruler's L-shaped name panel also frames his face and headdress. These two monuments are near mirror images conceived and designed as two halves of a scene.

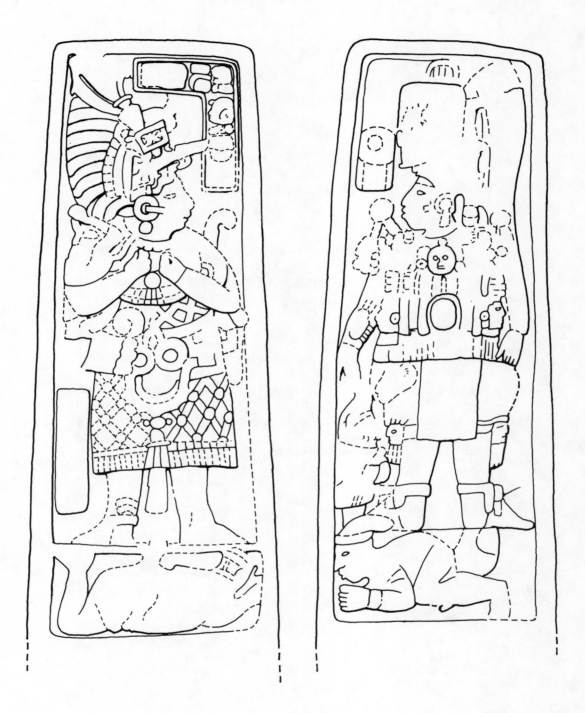

48. Two paired monuments (left, Stela 28; right, Stela 29) show the royal couple at A.D. 623. Beneath Ruler 2 (right) and his wife (left) are captive figures that face each other.

THE A.D. 642 - 652 COUPLE

Stela 88 is carved on all four sides; the male figure is apparently on the front and the female on the back, with texts on the sides. The stela is now broken into at least two large fragments (see Figure 60). Only the side showing the woman has been published; Ruppert and Denison (1943: Plate 53a) publish only the upper fragment, while Proskouriakoff (1950: Figure 42a) publishes both. This monument has been style-dated by Proskouriakoff (1950:185) to 9.11.0.0.0 $\pm$? *katuns* which means that its position in time might have to be adjusted as additional information is gathered.

THE A.D. 662 COUPLE

Stela 9 is unusual since it is carved from slate, and is extremely thin. While the height is close to three meters and the width half a meter, its thickness is only 15 centimeters. On the front of the stela is the male figure, with the female occupying the back. The male ruler stands atop four possible captive figures, two serving as pedestals under each foot (Ruppert and Denison 1943: Figure 48b). The ruler holds a shield in his left hand, and a short object in his right.

Four dates occur on Stela 9, but only one of them is not a period-ending date. That date is 9.10.16.16.19 (3 Cauac 2 Ceh), the Initial Series date on the left side. It is possible that this date concerns an event in the life of the woman, but I do not have sufficient data at this time to confirm it.

In large glyph blocks at the top of the back of the monument appears the Calendar Round date corresponding to August 21, A.D. 662 [9.11.10.0.0 (11 Ahau 18 Chen)]. The woman's name is given in two places -- in the panel of large glyph blocks (in the principal inscription) and in a panel of smaller hieroglyphs (incorporated as a band in her skirt). The terminal (or dedicatory) date of the monument is A.D. 672 [9.12.0.0.0 (10 Ahau 8 Yaxkin)].

THE A.D. 692 COUPLE

Two stelae of unknown provenience -- carved in a style similar to Calakmul's and apparently representing a royal marital pair -- were once set up near each other, but now lie far apart and out of their original context. The woman portrayed on Stela I is now in the Cleveland Museum of Art, and the man on Stela II is in the Kimbell Museum of Art in Forth Worth, Texas (see Figures 49 and 50). Unfortunately, we may never know whether the stelae are from Calakmul or elsewhere.

The woman's name is given in two separate cartouches in her headdress and again in the text at H2-H3 (see Figure 50). This text begins with a key event that took place on 9.12.13.13.5 2 Chicchan (8 Kayab). At B3-B4 is a passage that includes the verb "accession to the throne" or "receives the manikin scepter" (Marcus 1976b:134-135, 138; 1983a:471); a noun; and an emblem glyph which I suggested in 1973 might possibly be Calakmul's.

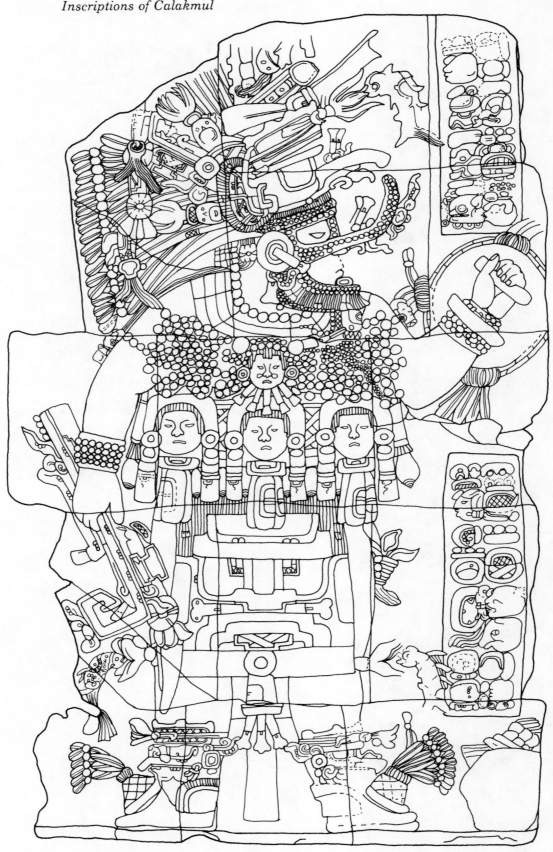

49. In A.D. 692, Stela II (above) and Stela I (Figure 50) were erected as a pair. This ruler's name is given in the panel near his face. A marriage bundle appears near his left foot (redrawn from Miller 1974: Figure 6).

50. Stela I gives the name of the ruler's wife in two cartouches in her headdress, and in the panel next to her left leg. (redrawn from Miller 1974: Figure 2).

For several reasons, Miller (1974) suggested that these

two monuments might be from Calakmul. One reason was the waist

motif (*xoc*, "shark" or "fish") worn by the woman on Stela I; the only

other example known to him was that worn by the woman on Stela 28

at Calakmul (Miller 1974:159). In addition, Miller considered a range

of other stylistic criteria. He emphasized that

> If St. I and St. II were acknowledged to come from Calakmul an unusual gap in the chronological record would be filled at this site. According to Denison's and Morley's reading of dates, there were four stelae erected at Calakmul on 9.12.0.0.0 (St. 9, 13, 32, 75), three at 9.14.0.0.0 (71, 72, 73), five at 9.15.0.0.0 (48, 52, 53, 54, 55), one on 9.16.0.0.0 (62), two at 9.17.0.0.0 (57, 58), one at 9.18.0.0.0 (80), and two at 9.19.0.0.0 (15, 16). It seems unlikely that none were erected to commemorate the 9.13.0.0.0 Katun anniversary, particularly when five stelae were dedicated on 9.13.10.0.0 (23, 24, 38, 40, 41).

> Lacking better alternatives at this moment, I would accept Marcus' identification of the fourth unknown emblem glyph at Copán as Calakmul. (Miller 1974:159-160)

While the date 9.13.0.0.0 is poorly represented on the

less eroded stelae at Calakmul, there are at least a couple of eroded

monuments that might have included that period-ending date (Morley in Ruppert and Denison 1943:119; Marcus 1970, 1983b). In fact, one of these (Stela 79) is cited by Miller himself.

THE A.D. 702 COUPLE

Still standing on the east side atop Structure VI (formerly called Structure F) is Stela 23, the woman associated with the male on Stela 24. The latter stela has since fallen. Between this marital pair is a small, plain altar, apparently shared. Both the male and female appear to stand on bound captives; the woman is garbed in a long dress.

Since both stelae were placed on the summit of Structure VI, it would seem that the altar, the stelae, and the structure were all dedicated on January 24, A.D. 702 [9.13.10.0.0 (7 Ahau 3 Cumhu)].

THE A.D. 731 COUPLE

Stelae 52 and 54 are set up on the west side of Structure I. Both commemorate the *katun* ending on August 20, A.D. 731 [9.15.0.0.0 (4 Ahau 13 Yax)]. These are two out of perhaps seven stelae that commemorate the end of the 15th *katun* and the reign of Ruler 7.

The woman on Stela 54 and the male on Stela 52 face each other (see Ruppert and Denison 1943: Figures 51c and 51a); both stand with feet at 180 degrees and wear similar sandals. Embedded within his elaborately feathered headdress is the hieroglyph for accession (perhaps commemorating his recent accession to the throne), while her headdress features the "fish nibbling water lily" motif. As we have noted above, marriage and accession to the throne both served as catalysts for the carving of royal couples at Calakmul.

Stela 52 shows Ruler 7 carrying a manikin scepter in his right hand and a shield in his left. His name and titles are given in two raised panels (one is in front of his headdress and the other is next to his left thigh). His wife also apparently holds a manikin scepter in her right hand and what appears to be a water lily in her left. This regally dressed pair is the last marital couple honored at Calakmul.

ROYAL WOMEN AT CALAKMUL

As many as five different women are portrayed on the Calakmul stelae (Marcus 1974a, 1976b:174). Given that the time span of these depictions was only 108 years (from A.D. 623 to A.D. 731), it is not surprising that they display significant similarities, most notably in attire which features long beaded skirts and elaborate feathered headdresses. Further, unlike most royal men at Calakmul, these royal women are associated with iconographic elements that emphasize "water symbolism"; this iconography includes various motifs such as fish nibbling water lilies, snails, shells, and flattened fish heads that clench large shells in their mouths. These "water" motifs are often included as part of the woman's headdress or worn around her waist. Not only do most royal women at Calakmul dress alike, so also do some of the royal women depicted on monuments at Calakmul's dependencies. However, among the dependencies, there are some exceptions -- for example, Stela 21 at Naachtún (Morley 1937: Volume V, Part 2, Plate 153c).

STELA 28

The earliest of the Calakmul monuments depicting women is Stela 28, dedicated on March 19, A.D. 623 (9.9.10.0.0) [see Figure 51]. On the front of the stela is a woman facing to her left, toward her husband on Stela 29 who in turn faces her (Figures 48). This woman wears an elaborate feathered headdress and a long beaded skirt that includes a rather crude version of the *xoc* motif -- the frontal view of a flattened fish head, clenching a *Spondylus* shell in its mouth -- at her waist (see Thompson's [1944] discussion of the *xoc* creature).

51. Stela 28, the first woman honored with her own monument at Calakmul.

As Miller (1974:154) and Thompson (1944, 1962) point out, the Maya term *xoc* can mean either "mythological fish" or "count"; in Yucatec it can also mean "hips" or "waist", which is exactly where this motif is worn by the royal women of Calakmul. Additionally, Miller states that in various highland Maya languages (such as Quiché, Cakchiquel, Tzutujil, Kekchi, Pokomam, and Pokomchi) *ixoc* means "señora" or "lady". Thus, Miller suggests that the *xoc* motif is a rebus for "waist" and "señora" -- that is, "a lady's waist".

The Stela 28 woman holds her arms in a position characteristic of much-earlier monuments (those carved in the Early Classic period), in which the arms are bent at the elbow and the fists are clenched against the center of the chest. In the crook of each elbow is a head held in the jaws of a serpent, which is part of a ceremonial bar. Below the woman's feet (which are splayed out at 180 degrees) is a separate register containing a captive figure, apparently lying face-down (see Figure 48). Two weathered hieroglyphic panels (one behind her, the other bracketing her headdress) supply us with parts of her name. At least one feminine head glyph occurs in the upper panel (see Figures 48 and 51). Texts on the sides of the stela are shown in Figures 52-55.

52. Text on left side of Stela 28.

53. Night photograph of the left side of Stela 28, showing the Initial Series date 9.9.10.0.0 (2 Ahau 13 Pop), which corresponds to March 19, A.D. 623.

54. Left side of Stela 28.

55. Right side of Stela 28.

STELA 9

A woman is depicted on the back of Stela 9, dedicated August 21, A.D. 662 [9.11.10.0.0 (11 Ahau 18 Chen)]. Her husband appears on the front face of the same monument. Like the "señora" on Stela 28, this woman wears a beaded skirt with a *xoc* motif at her waist. In contrast to Stela 28, however, the elements are not crudely done, even though they are somewhat eroded. A *Spondylus* shell, a nibbling fish, and part of a flattened fish head can be discerned. Atop her head is an elaborate headdress that includes a tied-up *Spondylus* shell with a water lily attached; a "snail"; a possible bone (?), and elements of the serpent bar. Her feet are also splayed out at 180 degrees. Below her sandals we see a separate register containing, on the left, a short text of five or six glyphs, and on the right, a captive.

56. Lower register on the back of Stela 9, showing the Calendar Round date of 13 Ahau 16 Yax (?), the date the captive shown here was taken by the woman portrayed in the register above.

57. On the back of Stela 9, this verb "was captured" is followed by this feminine head glyph, which forms part of the name of the woman portrayed in the register above. (From text in lower register.)

The text in this lower register begins with a date --
apparently intended to read 13 Ahau 18 Yax (?) [although it now looks
more like 16 Yax (?)] -- followed by the verb "was captured", and a
feminine head glyph postfixed by a few unclear hieroglyphic elements.
Thus, this text indicates that the woman --who is named and portrayed
in the register above -- had "captured" the figure depicted in the lower
register (see Figures 56 and 57).

Her name is given in two other places -- in the main
text (above her head) and in a band of eight hieroglyphs incorporated
into the lower part of her skirt (Figure 58). Of the eight glyphs, at
least six are "head" glyphs. Three of these are animal heads (one is
possibly a jaguar), and the remaining three are variants of the
"feminine head glyph" (see Figure 59).

STELA 88

Since the date on Stela 88 is so weathered, it is difficult to be precise about the dedicatory date. Proskouriakoff (1950: Figure 42a, 114, 185) was able to date it on stylistic grounds to A.D. 652 $\pm$ (?) [9.11.0.0.0 $\pm$ (?)]. This woman holds her arms in the same archaic position seen on Stela 28 (see Figure 60).

58. On the back of Stela 9, a band of hieroglyphs, giving the name of Ruler 3's wife, is incorporated into her skirt.

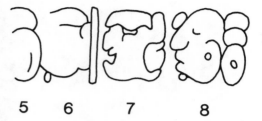

59. A band of hieroglyphs that gives the name of the woman on the back of Stela 9. Note three probable feminine head glyphs (at 1, 3, and 8) among the other head glyphs.

60. The woman portrayed on Stela 88 at Calakmul.

In the crook of each arm is the "grotesque" head of a supernatural. In her right arm, we see the head of an elderly, bald man with a superfix of the number 6, 7, or 8; in the crook of her left arm is a "God K" head with a superfix of the number 6, 7, or 8 and the sign for black + (?) (Ruppert and Denison 1943: Plate 53a).

This woman's attire is similar to that of the lady on Stela 9. She also wears a long beaded skirt with a large *xoc* at her waist and has her feet splayed out at the 180 degree position. In the lower register there may have been a captive, now eroded.

STELA I

Dating to March 16, A.D. 692 is Stela I, now housed in the Cleveland Museum of Art (see Figure 61; or frontispiece in Marcus 1976b; drawing first published by Miller 1974: Figure 2, and redrawn here as Figure 50). This woman is dressed in keeping with the attire typically worn by royal women at Calakmul, but the actual provenience of this stela is unknown (see pp. 135-136).

61. Stela I, showing an elaborately-dressed woman, who wears the xoc motif at her waist. (Photo courtesy of the Cleveland Museum of Art.)

She wears a beautifully-made ankle-length beaded skirt with a well-preserved and carefully-carved *xoc* motif at her waist. In the *xoc* creature's mouth (a *Spondylus* shell), three small hieroglyphs are incised. Like the woman on the back of Stela 9, she has her hieroglyphic name embedded in her clothing: however, unlike the woman on Stela 9 (whose name appeared as a band in her skirt), this woman's name occurs in her headdress. Among the feathers are two nearly-circular cartouches that give her name, which is also repeated in the main text (G2-H2). Among other events described in the main text, we find the accession of a ruler named "Jaguar Paw", who "received the manikin scepter", followed by an emblem glyph.

STELA 23

This woman, whose stela was dedicated ten years after Stela I, wears a long skirt with a beaded fringe at the bottom (Figure 62). A horizontal line of hieroglyphs is incorporated into the bottom of her skirt, very similar to the glyph band in the skirt worn by the woman on Stela 9.

62. Stela 23, a Calakmul woman.

63. Stela 23. Note the hieroglyphic band near the bottom of this woman's skirt; a similar hieroglyphic band was incorporated into the skirt worn by the woman on Stela 9 (see Figures 58 and 59).

Although eroded, four hieroglyphs are visible, at least one of which is a feminine head glyph (Figure 63). This clause appears to include the woman's name. She is shown standing with her feet positioned at the familiar angle of 180 degrees (Denison 1943:104).

STELA 54

This woman wears elaborate paraphernalia including a multi-strand collar or necklace of small jade plaques and a feather headdress with the "fish nibbling water lily" motif; she holds a water lily in her left hand, and a manikin scepter in her right. Her skirt is eroded, but there is the outline of what appears to be a *xoc* motif at her waist. Like other Late Classic royalty at Calakmul and elsewhere, she also has her feet positioned at an angle of 180 degrees. A narrow register occurs beneath her feet but its contents are not clear; it appears to be similar to the register beneath her husband's feet (on Stela 52). The woman's sandals also appear to be identical to her husband's (compare Stela 54 with 52 in Ruppert and Denison 1943: Plates 51a and 51c).

EMBLEM GLYPHS

Before embarking on a discussion of the emblem glyphs in the inscriptions at Calakmul, let us briefly review some of the results of past work dealing with emblem glyphs. For lengthier treatments of the subject, we refer the reader to earlier sources (Berlin 1958, 1977:87-90; Marcus 1973, 1974a, 1976b, 1984).

Most frequently, emblem glyphs are encountered in clauses that provide the names and titles of Maya lords; however, they may also occur in clauses that list "places". In some cases, emblem glyphs occur in clauses referring to four major "realms", regional capitals, or polities (Marcus 1973, 1976b, 1983a). Unfortunately, clauses of the latter type are known only for the Late Classic period (e.g. Stela A at Copán, Stela 10 at Seibal); the Copán clause lists four realms: Copán, Tikal, Calakmul (?), and Palenque. These Late Classic regional centers not only administered large realms, but they also were at the apex of well-developed regional hierarchies -- an important contrast with the Early Classic pattern.

While Berlin (1958:111), perhaps wisely, was noncommittal about the precise meaning of "glifos emblemas", he did offer a range of possible meanings (dynastic names, lineage names, tutelary deities, or site names). In my earlier research, I concluded that emblem glyphs functioned as geographical referents, which I loosely referred to as "site names" or "place names". Some emblem glyphs may refer to a unit as large as the whole realm, polity, or territory administered by a regional capital; others may be used in a more restricted or specific geographical context (Berlin 1977:87-88; Marcus 1974a, 1976b; Kelley 1976:215).

I consider it likely most emblem glyphs functioned as geographical referents -- and that they refer to the whole territorial unit or realm -- primarily because of the distribution pattern of emblem glyphs and the fact that most Mesoamerican Indians thought in terms of territorial units which included all the inhabitants that either owed allegiance to a particular ruler or labored periodically in the service of that ruler and his capital (Marcus 1983c:206-208). Such an area would extend well beyond the "downtown" of a Maya center, beyond its walls if it were a walled city, and beyond the high density of monumental plaza groups (and even not-so-monumental plaza groups). Such a realm might include lower-order centers (such as Chikin Tikal or Uolantún, for example) that never attain sufficient independence from the capital to acquire their own emblem glyphs. Since some capitals had more than one emblem glyph, I also considered it possible that one emblem glyph might have referred to the "site center" or "inner city" itself, while another was used to indicate the entire realm. The latter glyph could then be used by the capital, its dependencies located within that realm, and by other capitals in other realms.

Unfortunately, emblem glyphs are not numerous in the Calakmul inscriptions. One explanation may be that the severe weathering of the stelae has simply destroyed many that were originally present in the texts. In a future report on Calakmul in which more detailed epigraphic analyses will be presented, I hope to discuss a wider range of possible emblem glyphs. In this preliminary report, however, we will look at only a few of the more convincing emblem glyphs that occur.

On Stela 51, three possible emblem glyphs appear in the text (Figures 64 and 65a-c). Only one of the three (Figure 65a) appears to refer to Calakmul; the other two may refer to other places. A fourth emblem glyph (different from the three mentioned above) occurs on Stela 62 (Figure 65d). Still other emblem glyph candidates can be seen on Stelae 52, 64, 15, and 89.

An important emblem glyph (see Figure 65f) occurs in the inscriptions of the Cleveland Museum stela [thought by Miller (1974) to have been removed from Calakmul]. The same emblem glyph (main sign T-764 shown in Figure 65e; Thompson 1962) is also mentioned in the texts of Dos Pilas, Tikal, Copán, and Seibal (see Figure 65g, h, i, and j). At both Copán and Seibal, this glyph occurs as the third in a list of four emblem glyphs which appears to refer to the four major realms described as "on high" (Marcus 1973, 1976b, 1983a). In 1973 I suggested that this third realm might belong to "Calakmul (?)", deliberately attaching a question mark to it in recognition of the insufficient data available then. At the very least, it is clear from the context -- and the span of dates (A.D. 692 -- A.D. 849) covered by these stelae at Tikal, Copán, and Seibal -- that this emblem glyph has to refer to a very important Late Classic center which lasted into Cycle 10.

64. A name followed by a possible emblem glyph on Stela 51 (see Figure 65a). This is the close up of a short glyph panel next to Ruler 7's right leg, on the front of the stela.

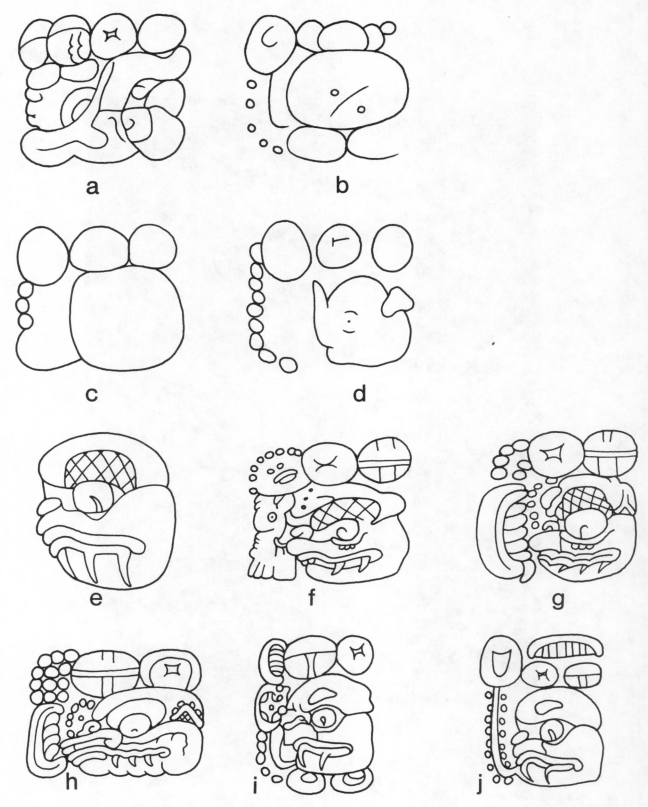

65. Emblem glyphs from various contexts. (a) Possible emblem glyph, panel near right leg of Ruler 7 (Stela 51, Calakmul). (b) Possible emblem glyph, incised near ruler's face (Stela 51, Calakmul). (c) Emblem glyph associated with captive (Stela 51, Calakmul). (d) Emblem glyph (Stela 62, Calakmul). (e) Main sign T-764 of emblem glyph. (f) Emblem glyph (Stela I). (g) Emblem glyph (Stela 13, Dos Pilas). (h) Emblem glyph (Lintel 3, Tikal). (i) Emblem glyph (Stela A, Copán). (j) Emblem glyph (Stela 10, Seibal).

In addition to the glyphs discussed above (some of which are shown in Figure 65), there are other candidates for emblem glyphs in the Calakmul inscriptions. Since none of these emblem glyphs occurs with sufficient frequency, however, it is difficult to make a strong case regarding which "city" or "realm" might be designated by each. With additional epigraphic work in the Calakmul realm -- particularly at Calakmul's dependencies -- and with research in nearby regions, in the future we may be in a better position to assign some of these emblem glyphs to particular localities.

A RESEARCH DESIGN FOR CALAKMUL

In spite of the numerous excavations carried out there, research in the Maya area is widely regarded as lagging behind that of other areas of Mesoamerica, where investigators have concerned themselves explicitly with the formulation of testable anthropological hypotheses and have adhered more closely to scientific research designs. Ironically, however, the Maya area is ideal for the formulation and testing of a wide range of anthropological hypotheses precisely because it affords us so many lines of evidence -- archaeology, iconography, epigraphy, and monuments dated to the exact day.

At a number of Maya sites, it is clear that specific structures (whether temples or palaces) were built by or for a specific ruler. Such associations are evident when the ruler's name is carved on the lintels or wall panels, because in both cases the hieroglyphic texts are incorporated into the building itself. In other cases, a tomb may be built for a specific ruler prior to the construction of the temple which stood above it. Because so many of Calakmul's monuments are still *in situ* -- linking specific rulers and their dated reigns to specific buildings which are still largely unexcavated -- the site seems unusually suited for a program of carefully-designed research. Such research could yield a chronology tied to the specific reigns of named rulers, whose contributions to the growth of the realm can be defined between Long Count dates.

We have seen that the time span of the stela groups placed in front of Calakmul's temples rarely exceeds that of a human lifetime; most, in fact, appear not to exceed the length of a reign. The time spans vary from as few as zero years (in the case of groups whose stelae all include the same dedicatory date) to groups which have dedicatory dates separated by as many as 40 years.

These spans of time -- all extremely short by archaeological standards -- lead us to hope that the dedication of each temple took place during the reign of the ruler whose monuments were set up before it; for if the dedications of stelae and temples were coincident, they can enable us to establish a much finer-grained chronological sequence. The ceramics associated with each temple could then be used to establish subphases, perhaps on the order of 100 years or even less. Since traditional Maya ceramic phases often span periods of 200 to 500 years, the establishment of shorter subphases within the Late Classic could produce the kind of sequence archaeologists often dream about when peering at the data ethnohistorians have at their disposal.

As far as we know, the span of time encompassed by all Calakmul monuments -- with the exception of Stela 43 -- falls within the Late Classic period. I therefore suggest that systematic excavation of the following structures, in the order indicated, might produce a fine-grained sequence of changes in architectural techniques and ceramic popularity which could be tied to Long Count dates.

1. Excavation of Structure V (A.D. 623?)

2. Excavation of Structure VIII (A.D. 634?)

3. Excavation of Structure IV

4. Excavation of Structure XV

5. Excavation of Structure XVIII (A.D. 672?)

6. Excavation of Structure XVI

7. Excavation of Structure IX (A.D. 682?)

8. Excavation of Structure VI

9. Excavation of Structure II (A.D. 702?)

10. Excavation of Structure I (A.D. 731?)

11. Excavation of Structure XIV (A.D. 741?)

12. Excavation of Structure XIII (A.D. 771?)

13. Excavation of Structure XVII (A.D. 790?)

14. Excavation of Structure X (A.D. 810?)

Our working hypothesis would be that the dedication of the temple, the stelae, and the ruler's reign coincide. If this is confirmed, it could result in a fine-grained sequence conforming closely to the order of the 14 excavations proposed above. If, on the other hand, such a chronological pattern should not be confirmed, we would have still learned something (cf. Ricketson and Ricketson 1937:154);

and we would then have to consider what other factors might have affected the timing of temple constructions, enlargements, and refurbishments. At the very least any additional inscriptions, tombs, or caches which came to light in the course of excavating the structures on the list above would assume greater significance because they would be given a context no random discovery can hope to have.

FUTURE RESEARCH AT THE REALM
LEVEL

Past Maya research has concentrated mainly on primary centers and intra-site patterns; much less attention has been devoted to site interactions within a political region, and the ways in which it can be documented. This intermediate level -- above that of the site and below that of the long-distance networks -- has yet to see its full potential tapped. Establishing the links between a primary center such as Calakmul and its lower-order dependencies is a difficult task, yet an important one, since it would give us information which could then be compared with the articulations of primary centers and their dependencies in other regions (such as those of Tikal, Palenque, and Copán).

At this writing, Folan and his mapping team have covered 30 square kilometers, beginning in "downtown" Calakmul;

their plan is to continue surveying until they reach at least some of the secondary centers. With this research strategy, it will be possible to see the settlement pattern of a region that functioned as a political unit. Excavation will be necessary both at lower-order centers and at the regional capital to answer many questions regarding the nature of the regional economy and sociopolitical organization. There are many fundamental aspects of this regional organization we do not know. For example, do capitals have types of buildings that are lacking at lower-order centers? Do capitals offer services and fulfill functions not performed by lower-order centers? Do capitals construct causeways to link themselves to their dependencies? Are the items produced at dependencies different from those produced at capitals? Is the production or distribution of goods at dependencies different from that at capitals? Is manpower organized differently within the realm? Do lower-order centers perform activities not carried out at capitals? The answers to all these questions should be yes, but we still do not know the full range of crafts and goods produced at lower-order centers (different types of pottery, eccentric flints, other tool types), nor do we know all the mechanisms integrating lower-order centers with regional capitals.

Of all the New World states, the Maya afford us one of the best opportunities for understanding the evolution, operation, and eventual fall of a complex society. Few other states offer such a variety of complementary data sets, including sixteenth-century descriptions of religion, social, and political organization; hieroglyphic inscriptions that span more than 600 years; regional settlement pattern data; intrasite evolution of plaza groups; deep, stratified deposits that provide architectural sequences; excellent glottochronological data; and data on subsistence and technology. The challenge is for us to integrate all these lines of evidence and to compare the Maya with other Mesoamerican states, to discover what they all share and how they differ in development and operation.

REFERENCES CITED

Acosta, Jorge R.

1977   Excavations at Palenque, 1967-1973. In *Social Process in Maya Prehistory: Studies in Honour of Sir Eric Thompson*, edited by Norman Hammond, pp. 265-285. Academic Press, London.

Adams, Richard E. W.

1977   Comments on the Glyphic Texts of the "Altar Vase". In *Social Process in Maya Prehistory: Studies in Honour of Sir Eric Thompson*, edited by Norman Hammond, pp. 409-420. Academic Press, London.

Adams, Richard E. W. and Richard C. Jones

1981   Spatial Patterns and Regional Growth among Classic Maya Cities. *American Antiquity*, Volume 46, pp. 301-322.

Adams, Richard E. W., W. E. Brown, Jr., and T. Patrick Culbert

1981   Radar Mapping, Archeology, and Ancient Land Use. *Science*, Volume 213, pp. 1457-1463.

Baudez, Claude

1978a   Segundo informe sobre las actividades del proyecto. Copán: Proyecto Arqueológico Copán.

1978b   Tercer informe sobre las actividades del proyecto. Copán: Proyecto Arqueológico Copán.

1979a   Cuarto informe sobre las actividades del proyecto. Copán: Proyecto Arqueológico Copán.

1979b   Quinto informe sobre las actividades del proyecto. Copán: Proyecto Arqueológico Copán.

Berlin, Heinrich

1955   News from the Maya World. *Ethnos*, Volume 20, Number 4, pp. 201-209. Stockholm.

1958   El Glifo "Emblema" en las Inscripciones Mayas. *Journal de la Société des Américanistes*, n. s., Tome XLVII, pp. 111-119. Paris.

1959   Glifos Nominales en el Sarcófago de Palenque: Un ensayo. *Humanidades*,
            Volumen II, Número 10, pp. 1-8. Universidad de San Carlos, Guatemala.

1960a   Mas Casos del Glifo Lunar en Números de Distancia. *Antropología e Historia
            de Guatemala*, Volumen XII, Número 2, pp. 25-33. Guatemala.

1960b   Pomoná, a New Maya Site (Preliminary Report). *Journal de la Société des
            Américanistes*, n.s., Tome XLIX, pp. 119-121. Paris.

1963   The Palenque Triad. *Journal de la Société des Américanistes*, n.s., Tome LII,
            pp. 91-99. Paris.

1965   The Inscription of the Temple of the Cross at Palenque. *American Antiquity*,
            Volume 30, Number 3, pp. 330-342.

1968a   The Tablet of the 96 Glyphs at Palenque, Chiapas, Mexico. *Middle American
            Research Institute*, Publication 26, pp. 135-150. Tulane University, New
            Orleans.

1968b   Estudios Epigráficos: II. *Antropología e Historia de Guatemala*. Volumen XX,
            Número 1, pp. 13-24. Guatemala.

1973   Beiträge zum Verständnis der Inschriften von Naranjo. *Bulletin de la Société
            Suisse des Américanistes*, No. 37, pp. 7-14. Musée d'Ethnographie, Genève.

1977   *Signos y Significados en las Inscripciones Mayas*. Instituto Nacional del
            Patrimonio Cultural de Guatemala, Guatemala, C.A.

1982   Tres Ensayos de Divulgación. *Historia y Antropología* de Guatemala:

Ensayos en Honor de J. Daniel Contreras R.*, edición preparada por Jorge

Luján Muñoz, pp. 1-13. Sección de Publicaciones, Facultad de Humanidades,

Universidad de San Carlos, Guatemala.

Carr, Robert F. and James E. Hazard

1961   Map of the Ruins of Tikal, El Petén, Guatemala. *Tikal Report, Number* 11.

University Museum Monographs, University Museum, University of

Pennsylvania, Philadelphia.

Clark, John E.

1984   *Calakmul Field Notes*. Manuscript in possession of author, Museum of

Anthropology, University of Michigan, Ann Arbor.

Coe, Michael D.

1956   The Funerary Temple Among the Classic Maya. *Southwestern Journal of

Anthropology*, Volume 12, Number 4, pp. 387-394.

Coe, William R.

1962   A Summary of Excavation and Research at Tikal, Guatemala: 1956-61.

American Antiquity, Volume 27, pp. 479-507.

1965a   Tikal, Guatemala, and Emergent Maya Civilization. *Science*, Volume 147,
         pp. 1401-1419.

1965b   Tikal: Ten Years of Study of a Maya Ruin in the Lowlands of Guatemala.
         Expedition, Volume 8, Number 1, pp. 5-56. University Museum, University
         of Pennsylvania, Philadelphia.

1967   *Tikal, A Handbook of the Ancient Maya Ruins.* University Museum,
         University of Pennsylvania, Philadelphia.

Demarest, Arthur A.

1984   Proyecto El Mirador de la Harvard University, 1982-1983. In *Mesoamérica,
         Publicación Semestral del Centro de Investigaciones Regionales de Mesoamérica*,
         Año 5, Cuaderno 7, pp. 1-13. Antigua, Guatemala and South Woodstock,
         Vermont.

Denison, John H., Jr.

1943   Description of the Monuments. In Archaeological Reconnaissance in
         Campeche, Quintana Roo, and Petén, by Karl Ruppert and John H. Denison,
         Jr. *Carnegie Institution of Washington, Publication* 543, pp. 99-154.
         Washington, D.C.

Domínguez Carrasco, María del Rosario

1986   Investigación Arqueológica en la Estructura VII de Calakmul, Campeche. *Información* 11, Centro de Estudios Históricos y Sociales, Universidad Autónoma del Sudeste, Campeche, México.

Fletcher, Laraine A., Jacinto May Hau, Lynda M. Florey Folan, and William J. Folan

1987   Un Análisis Estadístico Preliminar del Patrón de Asentamiento de Calakmul, Campeche, México. Universidad Autónoma del Sudeste, Campeche, México.

Folan, William J.

1985   Proyecto Calakmul. Su Centro Urbano, Estado y Región en Relación al Concepto del Resto de la Gran Mesoamérica. *Información* 9, pp. 161-185. Centro de Estudios Históricos y Sociales, Universidad Autónoma del Sudeste, Campeche, México.

Folan, William J. and Jacinto May Hau

1984   Proyecto Calakmul, 1982-1984: El Mapa. *Información* 8, pp. 1-14. Centro de Estudios Históricos y Sociales, Universidad Autónoma del Sudeste, Campeche, México.

Fry, Robert E. and Scott C. Cox

1974   The Structure of Ceramic Exchange at Tikal, Guatemala. *World Archaeology*, Volume 6, pp. 209-225.

Gallegos Gómora, Miriam Judith

1985   Excavaciones en la Estructura VII de Calakmul, Campeche. *Informe* para el Ing. Joaquín García Bárcena, Dirección de Monumentos Prehispánicos, México.

Gordon, George Byron

1896   Prehistoric Ruins of Copán, Honduras. A Preliminary Report of the Explorations by the Museum, 1891-1895. *Memoirs of the Peabody Museum of Archaeology and Ethnology, Harvard University*, Volume 1, Number 1. Cambridge.

Harrison, Peter D.

1977   The Rise of the *bajos* and the Fall of the Maya. In *Social Process in Maya Prehistory: Studies in Honour of Sir Eric Thompson*, edited by Norman Hammond, pp. 469-508. Academic Press, London.

Haviland, William A.

1967   Stature at Tikal, Guatemala: Implications for Ancient Maya Demography
and Social Organization. *American Antiquity*, Volume 32, pp. 316-325.

1970   Tikal, Guatemala, and Mesoamerican Urbanism. *World Archaeology*, Volume
2, pp. 186-198.

1977   Dynastic Genealogies from Tikal, Guatemala: Implications for Descent and
Political Organization. *American Antiquity*, Volume 42, pp. 61-67.

1981   Dower Houses and Minor Centers at Tikal, Guatemala: An Investigation
into the Identification of Valid Units in Settlement Hierarchies. In *Lowland
Maya Settlement Patterns*, edited by Wendy Ashmore, pp. 89-117. University
of New Mexico Press, Albuquerque.

Jones, Christopher

1977   Inauguration Dates of Three Late Classic Rulers of Tikal, Guatemala.
American Antiquity, Volume 42, pp. 28- 60.

Kelley, David H.

1962   Glyphic Evidence for a Dynastic Sequence at Quiriguá, Guatemala.
American Antiquity, Volume 27, Number 2, pp. 323-335.

1976   *Deciphering the Maya Script.* University of Texas Press, Austin.

Leventhal, Richard M.

1979   Settlement Patterns at Copán, Honduras. Unpublished doctoral dissertation,
            Harvard University, Cambridge, Massachusetts.

Longyear, J. M.

1952   Copán Ceramics: A Study of Southeastern Maya Pottery. *Carnegie
            Institution of Washington. Publication* 597. Washington, D.C.

Lundell, Cyrus Longworth

1933   Archaeological Discoveries in the Maya Area. *Proceedings of the American
            Philosophical Society*, Volume 72, Number 3, pp. 147-179. Philadelphia.

Marcus, Joyce

1970   *An Iconographic and Epigraphic Analysis of the Calakmul Monuments.*
            Manuscript in possession of author, Museum of Anthropology, University of
            Michigan, Ann Arbor.

1973   Territorial Organization of the Lowland Classic Maya. *Science*, Volume 180,
            pp. 911-916.

1974a   *An Epigraphic Approach to the Territorial Organization of the Lowland Classic Maya.* Doctoral dissertation, Harvard University, Cambridge, Massachusetts.

1974b   The Iconography of Power among the Classic Maya. *World Archaeology*, Volume 6, pp. 83-94.

1976a   The Origins of Mesoamerican Writing. *Annual Review of Anthropology*, Volume 5, pp. 35-67.

1976b   *Emblem and State in the Classic Maya Lowlands: An Epigraphic Approach to Territorial Organization.* Dumbarton Oaks, Washington, D.C.

1978   Archaeology and Religion: A Comparison of the Zapotec and Maya. *World Archaeology*, Volume 10, pp. 172-191.

1983a   Lowland Maya Archaeology at the Crossroads. *American Antiquity*, Volume 48, Number 3, pp. 454-488.

1983b   *Field Notes on the Calakmul Inscriptions.* Notebook in possession of author, Museum of Anthropology, University of Michigan, Ann Arbor.

1983c   On The Nature of the Mesoamerican City. In *Prehistoric Settlement Patterns: Essays in Honor of Gordon R. Willey*, edited by Evon Z. Vogt and Richard M. Leventhal, pp. 195-242. University of New Mexico Press, Albuquerque and Peabody Museum, Harvard University, Cambridge.

1984   Mesoamerican Territorial Boundaries: Reconstructions from Archaeology and Hieroglyphic Writing. *Archaeological Review from Cambridge*, Volume 3, Number 2, pp. 48-62. Department of Archaeology, Cambridge, England.

Matheny, Raymond T., editor

1980   El Mirador, El Petén, Guatemala: An Interim Report. *New World Archaeological Foundation*, *Paper* 45. Provo, Utah.

Miller, Jeffrey H.

1974   Notes on a Stelae Pair Probably from Calakmul, Campeche, Mexico. In *Primera Mesa Redonda de Palenque, Part I*, edited by Merle Greene Robertson, pp. 149-161. Robert Louis Stevenson School, Pebble Beach, California.

Morley, Sylvanus Griswold

1933   The Calakmul Expedition. *Scientific Monthly*, Volume 37, pp. 193-206. Lancaster, Pennsylvania.

1937-1938   The Inscriptions of Petén. *Carnegie Institution of Washington, Publication* 437, 5 volumes. Washington, D.C.

Proskouriakoff, Tatiana

1950   A Study of Classic Maya Sculpture. *Carnegie Institution of Washington,
Publication* 593. Washington, D.C.

1960   Historical Implications of a Pattern of Dates at Piedras Negras, Guatemala.
American Antiquity, Volume 25, Number 4, pp. 454-475.

1961a   The Lords of the Maya Realm. *Expedition*, Volume 4, Number 1, pp. 14-21.
University Museum, University of Pennsylvania, Philadelphia.

1961b   Portraits of Women in Maya Art. In *Essays in Precolumbian Art and
Archaeology*, edited by Samuel K. Lothrop *et al.*, pp. 81-99. Harvard
University Press, Cambridge.

1963   Historical Data in the Inscriptions of Yaxchilán, Part I. *Estudios de Cultura
Maya*, Volumen III, pp. 149-167. Universidad Nacional Autónoma de México,
México.

1964   Historical Data in the Inscriptions of Yaxchilán, Part II. *Estudios de Cultura
Maya*, Volumen IV, pp. 177- 201. Universidad Nacional Autónoma de
México, México.

1973   The *Hand-grasping-fish* and Associated Glyphs on Classic Maya Monuments. In *Mesoamerican Writing Systems: A Conference at Dumbarton Oaks, October 30th and 31st, 1971*, edited by Elizabeth P. Benson, pp. 165-178. Dumbarton Oaks, Washington, D.C.

Puleston, Dennis E.

1974   Intersite Areas in the Vicinity of Tikal and Uaxactún. In *Mesoamerican Archaeology: New Approaches*, edited by Norman Hammond, pp. 303-311. University of Texas Press, Austin.

Puleston, Dennis E. and D. W. Callender, Jr.

1967   Defensive Earthworks at Tikal. *Expedition*, Volume 9, Number 3, pp. 40-48. University Museum, University of Pennsylvania, Philadelphia.

Rands, Robert L. and Barbara C. Rands

1959   The Incensario Complex of Palenque, Chiapas, Mexico. *American Antiquity*, Volume 25, pp. 225-236.

Ricketson, Oliver G., Jr. and Edith B. Ricketson

1937   Uaxactún, Guatemala, Group E, 1926-1931. *Carnegie Institution of Washington, Publication* 477. Washington, D.C.

Ruppert, Karl

1943   Description of the Ruins. In Archaeological Reconnaissance in Campeche, Quintana Roo, and Petén, by Karl Ruppert and John H. Denison, Jr., pp. 13-96. *Carnegie Institution of Washington, Publication* 543, Washington, D.C.

Ruppert, Karl and John H. Denison, Jr.

1943   Archaeological Reconnaissance in Campeche, Quintana Roo, and Petén. *Carnegie Institution of Washington, Publication* 543. Washington, D.C.

Ruz Lhuillier, Alberto

1952a   Exploraciones en Palenque: 1950. *Anales*, Tomo V, pp. 25-45. Instituto Nacional de Antropología e Historia, México.

1952b   Exploraciones en Palenque: 1951. *Anales*, Tomo V, pp. 47-66. Instituto Nacional de Antropología e Historia, México.

1954   La Pirámide-Tumba de Palenque. *Cuadernos Americanos*, Volumen 75, pp. 141-159.

1955   Exploraciones en Palenque: 1952. *Anales*, Tomo 6, pp. 79-110. Instituto Nacional de Antropología e Historia, México.

1958a   Exploraciones arqueológicas en Palenque: 1953. *Anales*, Tomo X, pp. 69-116. Instituto Nacional de Antropología e Historia, México.

1958b   Exploraciones arqueológicas en Palenque: 1954. *Anales*, Tomo X, pp. 117-184. Instituto Nacional de Antropología e Historia, México.

1958c   Exploraciones arqueológicas en Palenque: 1955. *Anales*, Tomo X, pp. 185-240. Instituto Nacional de Antropología e Historia, México.

1958d   Exploraciones arqueológicas en Palenque: 1956. *Anales*, Tomo X, pp. 241-299. Instituto Nacional de Antropología e Historia, México.

1962   Exploraciones arqueológicas en Palenque: 1957. *Anales*, Tomo XIV, pp. 35-90. Instituto Nacional de Antropología e Historia, México.

1977   Gerontocracy at Palenque? In *Social Process in Maya Prehistory: Studies in Honour of Sir Eric Thompson*, edited by Norman Hammond, pp. 287-295. Academic Press, London.

Shook, Edwin M.

1960   Tikal Stela 29. *Expedition*, Volume 2, Number 2, pp. 29-35. University Museum, University of Pennsylvania, Philadelphia.

Shook, Edwin M., William R. Coe, Vivian L. Broman, and Linton Satterthwaite

1958   *Tikal Reports, Numbers* 1-4. Monographs of the University Museum, University of Pennsylvania, Philadelphia.

Spinden, Herbert J.

1916   Portraiture in Central American Art. In *Holmes Anniversary Volume: Anthropological Essays*, edited by Frederick W. Hodge, pp. 434-450. Washington, D.C.

Thompson, John Eric Sidney

1944   The Fish as a Maya Symbol for Counting and Further Discussion of Directional Glyphs. *Carnegie Institution of Washington, Division of Historical Research, Theoretical Approaches to Problems*, Number 2. Cambridge.

1962   *A Catalog of Maya Hieroglyphs*. University of Oklahoma Press, Norman.

Vogt, Evon Zartman

1964a   The Genetic Model and Maya Cultural Development. In *Desarrollo Cultural de los Mayas*, edited by Evon Zartman Vogt and Alberto Ruz Lhuillier, pp. 9-48. Universidad Nacional Autónoma de México, México.

1964b   Summary and Appraisal. In *Desarrollo Cultural de los Mayas*, edited by Evon Zartman Vogt and Alberto Ruz Lhuillier, pp. 385-403. Universidad Nacional Autónoma de México, México.

Willey, Gordon R.

1974   The Classic Maya Hiatus: "A Rehearsal" for the Collapse? In *Mesoamerican Archaeology: New Approaches*, edited by Norman Hammond, pp. 417-444. Duckworth, London.

1977   The Rise of Classic Maya Civilization: A Summary View. In *The Origins of Maya Civilization*, edited by Richard E. W. Adams, pp. 383-423. School of American Research Advanced Seminar Series, University of New Mexico Press, Albuquerque.

Willey, Gordon R. and Richard M. Leventhal

1979   Prehistoric Settlement at Copán. In *Maya Archaeology and Ethnohistory*, edited by Norman Hammond and Gordon R. Willey, pp. 75-102. University of Texas Press, Austin.

Willey, Gordon R., Richard M. Leventhal, and William L. Fash, Jr.

1978   Maya Settlement in the Copán Valley. *Archaeology*, Volume 31, pp. 32-43.